DIESEL, PARKING, & SERV.

Whether you're a truck driver or an RVer, we have a directory to meet your needs.

The Trucker's Friend®
THE NATIONAL TRUCK STOP DIRECTORY

4,800 US & Canadian truck stops and their services:

overnight parking lot size
diesel, gasoline, & propane motor fuel
restaurants, stores, & showers
load services, laundry, fax & lottery
scales, wash, repairs & road service
fuel cards and permit services

NOT SIMPLY AN EXIT GUIDE!

over 2,000 off-interstate diesel locations

guide to state agencies
state permit & over-dimensional guides
state fuel tax rates

The RVer's Friend™
GUIDE TO RV FRIENDLY TRUCK STOPS

4,800 US & Canadian truck stops and their services:

overnight RV parking
diesel, gasoline, & propane
restaurants & stores
laundry, fax & lottery
scales, wash, repairs & road service

NOT SIMPLY AN EXIT GUIDE!

over 2,000 off-interstate diesel locations

state & national parks
Army Corps of Engineers sites
rest areas with dump stations
state fuel tax rates

please send US$11.95 (includes 1st class postage) to:

TR Information
Department M
PO Box 476
Clearwater, FL 34617

or, put it on your Visa or MasterCard

800-338-6317

please specify whether you're a truck driver or an RVer

Serving Drivers since 1986

BANKS PUTS YOU IN THE FAST LANE!

Ford 460 & GM 454 Class 'A' and 'C' Motorhomes

Ford 460 & GM 454 Gasoline Trucks

Ford 6.9/7.3, GM 6.2/6.5 & Dodge 5.9 Cummins Diesel Trucks

Banks PowerPack®
DEEP-BREATHING POWER FOR GAS AND DIESEL ENGINES

With torque gains up to 99 lb.ft. and as many as 104 horses, you'll mow down those hills. Now, you can pull that gear with a lot less back-shifting and shrink merging distance by a football field.

Mix power with pleasure. Gain mileage without premium fuel, drop your engine temp and smile at the authoritative, yet civil, exhaust note.

Banks engineers and fabricates all his componentry to the highest standards, making installation a dream. Banks has a bullet-proof, 100% stainless or alumin-ized PowerPack System for your truck or motorhome.

Banks Sidewinder®
TURBOS PUMP UP DIESEL PICKUPS

With gains of up to 50% more horse-power and 40% greater torque, prepare to hang onto your hat! Banks has revolutionized turbocharger design with Sidewinder's larger, fast-acting turbine and high-capacity compressor. You get more miles-per-gallon, a cooler system and power right off idle ... No smoke!

CHEVY/GM 454 CARBURETED MOTORHOME ENGINE UTILIZING STAINLESS STAGE III POWERPACK

FORD 7.3L DIESEL ENGINE UTILIZING WASTEGATED SIDEWINDER TURBO

TIME TO CHANGE LANES!
For a FREE Test Report, Call
1 800 GET POWER
(800) 438-7693 • (818) 969-9605 • FAX (818) 334-8087

© 1996 Gale Banks Engineering

Gale Banks Engineering • 546 Duggan Avenue Dept. 605, Azusa, CA 91702 • (M-F) 7am-6pm (SAT) 9am-1pm, PST

MOUNTAIN DIRECTORY
for
TRUCKERS, RV, AND MOTORHOME DRIVERS

*Locations and Descriptions
of over 250 Mountain Passes and Steep Grades
in Eleven Western States*

Acknowledgments

A word of thanks must be extended to all of the people who helped during the gathering of information for this publication. Highway Patrol officers and Department of Transportation employees in eleven states were always helpful and informative about where to find the longest and steepest hills. In addition, there is a new section in the back of the book that includes pass and grade information contributed by readers. This type of information is most welcome and will be passed along. Please write or call if you are aware of grades that should be included in the book. Address and phone number below.

All maps included in this publication were made with MapInfo® software from MapInfo Corporation, Troy, New York.

Front cover photo: Going to the Sun Road, Glacier National Park, Montana.
Back cover photo: View from Colorado Highway 82 west of the summit of Independence Pass.
Both photos by Richard Miller.

Boxes like this are provided for notetaking and are also available as advertising space for truck stops, RV dealers or repairshops, equipment suppliers to the trucking or RV markets, RV resorts, etc. For more information call I-913-594-4054, or write to:
Mountain Directory
R&R Publishing Inc.
PO Box 941
Baldwin City KS 66006

To order additional copies of this book please call 1-800-594-5999.

ISBN: 0-9646805-1-3

MOUNTAIN DIRECTORY is published by R&R Publishing Inc.
© Copyright 1996 by R&R Publishing Inc.
PO Box 941
Baldwin City, Kansas 66006
1-913-594-4054

All rights reserved. No use is permitted which will infringe the copyright without the express written consent of the publisher. No part of this book may be reproduced, stored or transmitted by any means without prior written permission from the publisher. All information contained in this book has been obtained from sources believed to be reliable. But because of the possibility of errors and changes in roadways or conditions, R&R Publishing Inc. assumes no responsibility for its accuracy or completeness.

POLICY: All advertisements are accepted and published by R&R Publishing Inc. upon the representation that the advertiser and its advertising company, if any, is authorized to publish the contents thereof. The publisher has not investigated the claims of the advertisers and advertising companies and makes no warranty express or implied regarding the accuracy of such advertisements contents.

INTRODUCTION

In most cases the passes and hills described in this book are described as descents. In other words, a pass will be described from the summit down in one direction and then from the summit down in the other direction. As anyone who has ever lost their brakes on the downhill side of a mountain can tell you, it is the descent that is the most dangerous. Of course, the long and steep climbs have their own set of problems, too.

This directory does not claim to include every steep grade. In fact, we can guarantee that we have missed some. Many times the percentages quoted are estimates and many times they are based on road signs or information provided by highway departments.

This book does not attempt to rate mountain passes or steep grades according to difficulty. There is an enormous variety in vehicles and equipment. A hill that is very difficult for one vehicle may be no problem at all for a similar vehicle that is equipped differently. Driver judgement is critical in deciding which hills should be avoided.

At the end of the Colorado section, (pages 45, 46, and 47) there is some information supplied by the Colorado Department of Transportation, The Colorado Motor Carriers Association, and the Colorado State Patrol. We thank these organizations for providing this material and giving their permission to include the material in this book. Much of the information would apply to any steep grade regardless of it's location. The pages are a reproduction of a brochure entitled **"Runaway Truck Ramps"** that was completed and issued in 1986, but most of the information should still apply. There are several statistics about runaway truck ramp usage that may be different today, but the brochure reveals some interesting facts:

* 62% of the runaway trucks using the ramps are registered in states east of Colorado. (This means that 38% are registered in western states.)

* 37% of the drivers utilizing the ramps have less than one year of mountain driving experience. (So 63% are veteran mountain drivers!)

* 55% of the vehicles entering the ramps were in the 70 to 80 thousand pound gross vehicle weight range. (So 45%, or almost half, were under 70,000 pounds.)

These statistics will probably surprise many drivers.

The purpose of the information in this book is not to discourage drivers from going where they please. It is only to inform them of the conditions they may encounter. Whether or not they make the trip must be left to the driver's own judgment. This is an encouragement to drivers to make sure their equipment is in good repair. Brakes must be in good working order and proper adjustment and the engine and transmission should be used to slow the vehicle whenever possible, thus saving the brakes and keeping them cool enough to retain their stopping power. The vehicle's engine cooling system needs to be in good working order to prevent overheating during the climbs. Turning off the air conditioning during the climbs may help, and if necessary, turning on the heater will help dissipate heat from the engine. Weather must also be considered when driving in the mountains.

Some passes are marked with speed limits according to the weight of the vehicle. One of these is Homestake Pass outside of Butte, Montana. The highway department has posted a 25 mph speed limit for vehicles over 12,000 lbs for the eastbound descent. This, along with a warning sign at the top of the pass, has resulted in fewer truck accidents on this pass. Another grade with speed limits according to weight is Cabbage Hill in Oregon. The highway department has posted these speed limits:

5 axles or more:

weight (lbs.)	speed limit
60,000 to 65,000	37 mph
65,000 to 70,000	26 mph
70,000 to 75,000	22 mph
75,000 to 80,000	18 mph

These guidelines would be appropriate on many grades for many vehicles. Don't forget that while RV's and motorhomes may weigh less than tractor trailer rigs, they also have fewer brakes and smaller brake shoes and pads. Keeping brakes properly and evenly adjusted is extremely important.

There are many aftermarket devices that can help heavy vehicles in the mountains. Some will help by increasing horsepower for the climbs. These include turbos and exhaust systems. Other devices, such as engine braking systems can help in the descents. Some products like gear splitters and auxiliary transmissions can help during the climb *and* the descent. Many of these products also improve fuel economy (while delivering more horsepower) and reduce wear and tear on the drive train.

The main ingredients involved in overheated brakes are length of the grade, steepness of the grade, speed and weight of the vehicle. Reducing any of these will improve the chances of getting down the mountain without overheating the brakes. Most of the time the only one the driver can change is speed. Reducing speed may keep you alive. Remember the old phrase, *"You can go down a mountain a thousand times too slowly, but only once too fast."*

INDEX

ARIZONA	1
CALIFORNIA (NORTHERN)	11
CALIFORNIA (SOUTHERN)	23
COLORADO	31
IDAHO	49
MONTANA	57
NEVADA	65
NEW MEXICO	75
OREGON	81
UTAH	95
WASHINGTON	101
WYOMING	109
ADDITIONAL INFORMATION AND READER INPUT	116
NEW PASS & GRADE INFORMATION	117

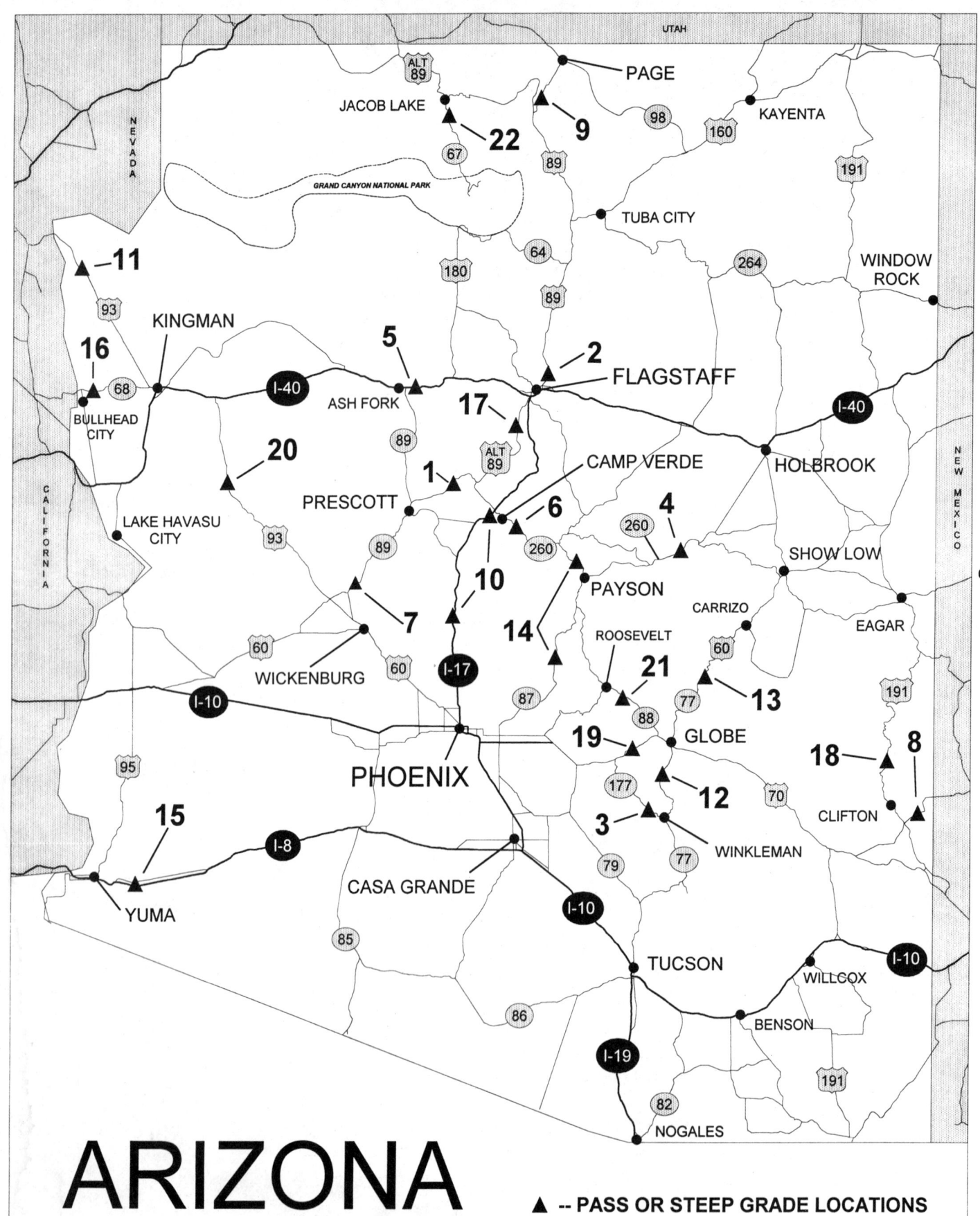

ARIZONA

▲ -- PASS OR STEEP GRADE LOCATIONS

ARIZONA

ARIZONA

1. US HIGHWAY 89 ALT.
2. US HIGHWAY 89
3. ARIZONA HIGHWAY 177
4. ARIZONA HIGHWAY 260
5. I-40 NEAR ASH FORK
6. ARIZONA HIGHWAY 260 (near CAMP VERDE)
7. ARIZONA HIGHWAY 89
8. ARIZONA HIGHWAY 78
9. US HIGHWAY 89
10. CAMP VERDE GRADES and I-17
11. HOUSEHOLDER PASS
12. EL CAPITAN PASS
13. SALT RIVER CANYON
14. ARIZONA HIGHWAY 87
15. TELEGRAPH PASS
16. UNION PASS
17. US HIGHWAY 89 ALT.
18. US HIGHWAY 191 (666)
19. US HIGHWAY 60
20. US HIGHWAY 93

21 & 22 see New Info on page 117

Miscellaneous notes for Arizona:
There could be some confusion about highways 89 and 89 Alt. because some maps show them as State highways and some maps show them as US highways. North of I-40 they all seem to agree that they are US highways.

Between Flagstaff and Prescott, 89 Alt. is shown as a US highway on some maps and a State highway on other maps. The exit from I-17 south of Flagstaff calls it US 89 Alt.

Between Ash Fork and Wickenburg, some maps show State 89 and some show US 89.

Between Phoenix and Tucson, (thru Florence Jct. and Florence) some maps show US 89 and some maps show State 79 (yes, 79 not 89).

1 US HIGHWAY 89 ALT.
(between US 89 and Clarkdale, Az)

Trucks over 50' in length prohibited. This road is narrow and winding with sharp curves and very tight hairpin turns.

About 7 1/2 miles south of Jerome US highway 89 Alt. comes to a summit. The southbound descent from the summit is about **4 1/2 miles of 6-7% grade** with many 20 and 30 mph curves and a 15 mph hairpin near the top. There are about 2 miles of 4% grade after the steep section.

The northbound descent is about **12 miles of 6% grade** with narrow road and many 20 mph curves and several 15 mph hairpin turns. The town of Jerome is about 7 miles down from the summit. Jerome is perched on the side of the mountain and the road is very narrow thru town and includes a very sharp 10 mph hairpin turn and a short section of about **10 or 12% downhill grade**. After leaving town there are **3 1/2 miles of 6%** grade with sharp turns. The grade eases when US 89 Alt. turns southeast toward Cottonwood.

ARIZONA

2 US HIGHWAY 89
(north of Flagstaff, AZ)

About 10 miles north of the Flagstaff city limit there is a northbound descent on US 89. Near milepost 431 there is a sign for northbound traffic--**"6% grade next 4 miles."** The last mile or so may be less than 6%.

3 ARIZONA HIGHWAY 177
(between Kearny and Superior, AZ)

There are rolling hills between Superior and Kearny, but none of them last very long. There are **10% grades** posted for both northbound and southbound traffic, but none over 2 miles in length.

About milepost 161 there is a hill posted **10% 2 miles** for southbounders and **10% 1 mile** for northbounders. About milepost 158 there is a hill posted **10% 1 mile for both directions.** About milepost 154 1/2 there is a hill for southbound traffic posted at **10% 2 miles**. There is almost no descent for northbounders.

4 ARIZONA HIGHWAY 260
(between Heber and Payson, AZ)

There are two descents of some length for westbound traffic on this part of 260. At milepost 282 there is a brake check area and warning sign--**"Trucks--vehicles pulling trailers check brakes and equipment."** This is about 22 miles west of Heber. The grade is **steady 6% for 5 miles** with 45 mph curves. The road is 4 lane during the descent.

The other long hill starts at milepost 265 and is **3 1/2 miles of 6% grade.** There are some places where the grade eases for short stretches. There are 40 and 45 mph curves and the road is 2 lane. There are plenty of other 5 and 6% hills along this road but they are usually short.

5 I-40 NEAR ASH FORK

About 10 miles east of Ash Fork there is a brake check area for westbound traffic (near milepost 155 1/2) and some warning signs--**"Trucks--vehicles pulling trailers check brakes and equipment--use lower gear"** and **"6% grade next 6 miles."**

The **first 2 miles are 6%** followed by about 1 1/2 miles of 4-5% and 1 1/2 miles of 6% grade.

6 ARIZONA HIGHWAY 260
(between Arizona highway 87 and Camp Verde, AZ)

About 14 1/2 miles west of the junction of 87 and 260 highways there is a sign--**"6% grade next 9 miles."** The westbound descent begins 1/4 mile later at milepost 238.

The **first 3 1/4 miles are steady 6-7% grade** with 45 and 50 mph curves. The grade eases for about 3/4 mile and then goes back to **6-7% for almost 5 miles** and then eases to 3-4% for 1 mile. The grade then goes back to **6% for 1 mile** and flattens out about milepost 227, which is 11 miles down from the top. There are 45 mph curves all the way down. It is a good 2 lane road.

This hill is long and steep--use caution in large or heavy vehicles. There are no escape ramps on this hill. This descent is more dangerous than many hills that do have escape ramps.

7 ARIZONA HIGHWAY 89
(between US 93 and Prescott, AZ)
"Not recommended for trucks pulling trailers over 40' long."

Just south of Yarnell, Arizona there is a descent for traffic going south on 89. The descent is about **5 1/2 miles of 5-6% grade** with many 25 and 30 mph curves and a couple of 20 mph hairpin turns. The road is 4 lane at the top but soon splits--northbound and southbound are at different elevations--and the downhill side becomes one lane until the bottom of the hill.

Farther north on 89 is the town of Wilhoit, Arizona. From Wilhoit to Prescott the road has **many curves that are too tight for large trucks.** *The guardrail is damaged at almost every curve (where there is a guardrail).* The grade is up and down for the entire 15 mile stretch. Some of the grade is in the 6% range--both up and down--but it never does last for very long. The curves do last--all the way across there are 20 and 25 mph curves--hardly a straight stretch at all.

8 ARIZONA HIGHWAY 78
(between Threeway, AZ and Mule Creek, NM)

This road is posted--"Curves--mountain grades--trucks not recommended."

Highway 78 is a narrow, winding road with 15 mph hairpin turns and many 20-30 mph curves. The summit of the hill is about milepost 168 1/2 (about 5 1/2 miles west of the state line).

The westbound descent starts with about **4 miles of steady 7-8% grade** with 25 mph curves. After that it is a roller coaster descent for about 7 miles with grades that vary from 4-7% and almost constant 25 mph curves. The eastbound descent rolls up and down with short 5 and 6% grades and numerous 20 and 25 mph curves.

9 US HIGHWAY 89
(between Page and Bitter Springs, AZ)

Southbound traffic out of Page, Arizona will encounter some warning signs near milepost 528-**"Trucks--vehicles pulling trailers check brakes and equipment"** and **"use lower gear next 5 miles."** About 1/2 mile later there is a brake check area and the grade starts down at about 6% with 45 mph curves. The grade is **4 miles of steady 6%.**

There is a *runaway truck ramp about milepost 524 1/2* which is about 3 1/4 miles down from where the 6% grade started. The escape ramp exits to the right and goes slightly downhill. The grade eases about 1/2 mile past the escape ramp near the junction of 89 and 89 Alt.

3

ARIZONA

10 CAMP VERDE GRADES and I-17
(between Flagstaff and Phoenix, AZ)

Camp Verde, Arizona is in a valley and the descent is long and steep from both north and south on I-17. **There are runaway truck ramps on both of these hills.** There is also a steep descent for southbounders near Black Canyon City between mileposts 251 and 244 on I-17.

FROM THE NORTH INTO CAMP VERDE:

About 26 miles south of the junction of I-40 and I-17 at Flagstaff there is a sign for southbound traffic--**"6% grade 2 miles ahead."** About 1/2 mile later is another sign--**"Trucks--vehicles pulling trailers check brakes and equipment--use senic view."** At milepost 312 a sign warns--**"6% grade next 13 miles"** and 1/2 mile later the 6% begins. The **first 3 1/2 miles are fairly steady 6% grade.**

There are several breaks in the descent where the grade eases. The first two breaks are only 1/4 to 1/2 mile long and then between mileposts 306 and 304 the grade is about 4%. **Between mileposts 304 and 298 the grade is pretty steady at 6% (almost 6 miles). There is a runaway truck ramp just before milepost 300.** The ramp goes off to the right and is almost level. There are several warning signs as you approach it.

About milepost 298 the grade goes uphill for a short distance and then flattens as you approach the rest area. If your brakes are hot this may be a good place to cool them because it is still 9 miles to the bottom of the hill at Camp Verde. Not all of the 9 miles are downhill--in fact there is a mile of uphill included-- and most of the downhill is 4-5% from the rest area to Camp Verde.

FROM THE SOUTH INTO CAMP VERDE:

At milepost 280 1/2 on I-17 there is a brake check pullout and then a sign for northbounders--**"6% grade next 7 miles"** and *"Runaway truck ramp LEFT 2 1/4 miles."*

The 6% grade starts down at *milepost 281 and is steady for all but a little of the 7 miles.* The runaway truck ramp is at milepost 283. The road curves to the right and the escape ramp goes straight from the *left lane* and uphill. The grade eases to 4-5% for the last mile into Camp Verde.

FROM THE NORTH INTO BLACK CANYON CITY:

At milepost 253 there is a sign for southbounders--**"Trucks--vehicles pulling trailers check brakes and equipment--use rest area."** After coming out of the rest area there are signs stating-**"winding road"** and **"6% grade next 5 miles."**

At milepost 251 the 6% grade begins with 60 mph curves. After 2 1/2 miles the grade eases for 1/2 mile and then goes back to 6% for 2 miles. It eases again for about 3/4 mile and then is 4-5% for another mile or so to the exit for Black Canyon City.

11 HOUSEHOLDER PASS and BOULDER DAM AREA
(on US 93 between Kingman, AZ and Boulder Dam)

If you are traveling north on US 93 from Kingman to Boulder Dam the last 16 miles before reaching the dam are a roller coaster ride. There are uphill grades and downhill grades that range from 2% to 6%. The **last 6 miles, starting at milepost 6 1/2 are mostly 5-6% downgrade.** The road becomes very curvy and steep near the dam with 15 and 25 mph curves as you turn onto the dam.

From Boulder City, Nevada toward the dam there is a hill about 3 miles long at 4-5% and then the grade eases for about a mile before going to 5-6% the last 2 miles to the dam. There are 15 mph curves near the bottom of the hill.

ARIZONA

12 EL CAPITAN PASS elev. 4983'
(on Arizona Highway 77 between Globe and Winkelman, AZ)

The summit of El Capitan Pass is about 8 1/2 miles south of the junction of US 70 and Arizona 77 highways (about milepost 162 1/2). There is a brake check area at the top. There are warnings posted for traffic in both directions--**"Trucks--vehicles pulling trailers check brakes and equipment."**

The northbound descent begins with a sign--**"8% grade next 3 miles."** The grade eases some after 2 miles but starts down at about 6% a mile later. The 6% lasts for about a mile for a total descent of about 4 miles. The road rolls along the top of the pass for about 1 1/2 miles and the southbound descent begins about milepost 161. There is a brake check area following the usual warnings about checking equipment.

The southbound descent begins with a sign--**"7% grade next 7 miles."** The last 2 miles of this hill are posted at **8% grade**. The descent is fairly steady with 45 mph curves. *There are two runaway truck ramps. The first is at milepost 156 and the second is 1 1/2 miles farther down the hill.* They are 4 3/4 and 6 1/4 miles down from the top of the pass. In both cases the road makes a curve to the left and the escape ramp exits straight ahead. **The 8% grade continues for about 1 mile after the second escape ramp.** There are some rolling hills after that with a few short 5-6% descents.

13 SALT RIVER CANYON
(and US 60 between Show Low and Globe, AZ)

The northbound trip from Globe to Show Low on US 60 includes several long uphill grades and one long descent. There are many short hills scattered all along the way.

The long northbound descent is into Salt River Canyon. It begins at milepost 284 with a sign--**"6% grade next 3 miles."** *What that sign doesn't tell you is that after a one mile break in the grade there is another sign--***"6% grade next 5 miles"** *so you have* **a total of 8 miles of 6% grade** *going into the canyon.* The grade is steady except for the one mile break and there are 50 mph curves during the first 3 miles and 25 and 35 mph curves during the last 5 miles.

The southbound trip from Show Low to Globe has four long, steep descents and the long pull out of Salt River Canyon. About 32 miles south of Globe at milepost 307 1/2 a **7 mile descent** begins. The **grade is mostly 5-6% and is not steady.** The grade stairsteps down with short flat spots or stretches of lesser grade. *You want to avoid overheating your brakes during this section because about 2 miles after it bottoms out the descent into Salt River Canyon begins.*

About milepost 298 1/2 there is a brake check area and the **5 1/2 mile 6% grade** into the canyon begins. It is **steady 6%** except for a 1/2 mile section of 3-4% in the middle. There are many 25, 30, and 35 mph curves. After you have climbed out of the canyon on the south side there are two more long descents before reaching Globe. Near milepost 279 there is a sign for southbound traffic--**"6% grade next 8 miles."** There are three short sections where the grade eases, the longest is about a mile of 4-5% in the middle of the grade.

The last long hill begins about milepost 262 where there is a sign--**"6% next 3 miles."** The grade is closer to 5 miles long but is not steady. The grade stairsteps down with 6% alternating with 4%.

Instant Power You can FEEL! Improves Acceleration, Hill Climbing & Passing!

GIBSON PERFORMANCE EXHAUST SYSTEMS

Complete Exhaust Systems...from Headers to Stainless Steel tip
TRUCKS and MOTORHOMES! • Lowest Price/Highest Quality
Aluminized & Stainless Bolt-on Kits • 50 State Legal • Lifetime Warranty

GIBSON PERFORMANCE EXHAUST SYSTEMS

714/528-3044 • **FREE CATALOG** • 800/528-3044

ARIZONA

14 ARIZONA HIGHWAY 87
(between Phoenix and Long Valley, AZ)

The community of Payson is about milepost 253 on highway 87. Just south of Payson at milepost 250 a descent begins for southbounders. There are two short sections of 6-7% grade during the next 2 miles and at milepost 248 there is a sign--**"Trucks--vehicles pulling trailers check brakes and equipment--1/4 mile."** There is a brake check pullout and then **5 1/2 miles of 6-7% grade** with only a couple of short breaks in the grade. There are 45 mph curves. After the steep section a mile or so of 3% grade takes you into Rye, Arizona.

Between Rye and Phoenix there are many 5, 6, and 7% grades with climbs and descents whichever way you are traveling. There is a 3 mile 7% hill and a 4 mile 6% hill and a 2 mile 7% hill and everything in between. It is a good 2 land road with passing lanes on most of the climbs. From Payson southbound for about 30 miles is 4 lane.

There is another long descent on this road. About 24 miles north of Payson is the junction of 87 and 260 highways. About 1 1/2 miles south of the junction a descent begins for southbounders. The first 2 1/2 miles are mostly 3-4% downhill. At this point there is a brake check pullout (milepost 274 1/2). Then the grade starts down at about **6% for 4 miles into the town of Strawberry.** There are 20, 30, 35, and 40 mph curves. **After passing thru Strawberry the grade resumes for another 3 miles to the town of Pine.** Between Pine and Payson there are short ups and downs in the grade--some steep but short. There are also some short and steep hills for about 10 miles north of the junction with 260.

15 TELEGRAPH PASS elev. 1980'
(on I-8 east of Yuma, AZ)

The eastbound descent from the summit (milepost 19) of Telegraph Pass is **6% grade for 2 miles** with a truck speed limit of 45 mph. There are 45 mph curves.

The westbound descent from the summit is also about **2 miles of 5-6% grade.**

16 UNION PASS elev. 3600'
(on Arizona Highway 68 between Kingman and Bullhead City, AZ elev. 675')

The westbound descent from the summit of Union Pass is **almost 12 miles of 6% grade** with a 45 mph curve at the bottom that is at the outskirts of Bullhead City. *Use caution on this hill.*

About 1/2 mile down from the summit is a sign-**"6% grade next 9 miles."** There is a **runaway truck ramp 10 miles from this sign** and the grade continues another 1 1/4 miles past the escape **ramp** and begins to flatten out about the time you go thru the 45 mph curve. *(There is a drop in elevation of almost 3000' from Union Pass Summit to Bullhead City.)*

The eastbound descent from Union Pass Summit is about 1 mile of 6% grade followed by about 4 miles of 4% grade.

ARIZONA

17 US HIGHWAY 89 ALT
(between Flagstaff and Sedona, AZ)

"Trucker's notice--US 89 A not recommended for heavy trucks." This sign calls the road US 89 A but some maps show it as a state highway.

From the junction of I-17 and US 89 A just south of Flagstaff the road rolls up and down and descends gradually for about 8 1/2 miles. At this point (about milepost 390.5) there is a sign for southbounders--**"7% grade next 3 miles."** There are many curves including several 15 mph hairpin turns. The road is also very narrow. After the 3 miles of 7% the grade is variable and rolling but continues to descend gradually for about 11 miles. There are some 5 and 6% sections but they are usually short. The road continues to be narrow and winding.

18 US HIGHWAY 191 (formerly known as US 666)
(between Clifton and Alpine, AZ)

From 5 miles south of Hannagan Meadow to the north side of Morenci is **prohibited to trucks over 40' in length.** There is also a **tunnel** just north of Morenci with a **12' 7" vertical clearance.**

This road is not suitable for large vehicles from Morenci to just south of Hannagan Meadow. The grades can be as steep as 8 or 9% but they are usually short. The road is extremely narrow in many places with an incredible number of 10 and 15 mph hairpin turns not to mention many 20 and 25 mph curves. The first 20 miles north of Morenci takes over an hour in a car.

About 6 1/2 miles south of Hannagan Meadow, there is a **steady 6% southbound descent for about 5 miles** with 20 mph curves.

There is a short 6% descent from Morenci to Clifton and a 2 mile 6% climb out of Clifton going southbound.

19 US HIGHWAY 60
(between Miami and Superior, AZ)

There is very little flat road between Miami and Superior. There are **6 and 7% descents for traffic in both directions.** There is a **tunnel with 14' 0" vertical clearance** about 2 miles east of Superior. About milepost 236 there is a sign for eastbounders--**"6% grade next 7 miles."** This descent toward Miami is not a steady 6%. There are several places where the grade eases and there is a 1 mile uphill stretch. There is still enough 6% descent to require caution on this road. There are 45 mph curves and heavy traffic. At the bottom of the hill is Miami.

The westbound descent from milepost 236 starts with about 2 miles of 3-4% grade and then **2 miles of 6% grade.** At this point there is a 1/2 mile 6% climb before beginning a descent of **1 mile of 5% followed by 3 miles of 7% grade.** There are 50 mph curves all the way down and a *runaway truck ramp at milepost 228.* It exits to the right and goes uphill.

About **1 1/4 miles of 7% grade remain after the escape ramp.** This brings you to the edge of Superior where the grade goes to 4% right thru town.

Note: If you are traveling eastbound there is a sign near milepost 231 1/2 that says--**"6% next 12 miles."** Evidently this includes uphill grade as well as down because after going downhill for about 1/2 mile the grade is uphill for 4 1/2 miles and then downhill for 7 miles into Miami.

ARIZONA

20 US HIGHWAY 93
(south of I-40 in western AZ)

There is a great deal of traffic on this road--including a lot of truck traffic. Between I-40 and Wikieup, Arizona there are rolling hills. From Wikieup, about milepost 123, south to milepost 160 there are many 5-6% grades both uphill and downhill. These grades are not usually steady but stairstep up or down and can add up to a considerable length--as much as 5 or 6 miles. This section is also quite curvy.

From milepost 161 to milepost 172 is a long straight pull for southbounders or long descent for northbound traffic. Most of the grade is 3-4%.

The state of Arizona has marked fatal accident sites with white crosses and there are a number of them on this road.

21 and 22 see New Info on page 117.

ARIZONA

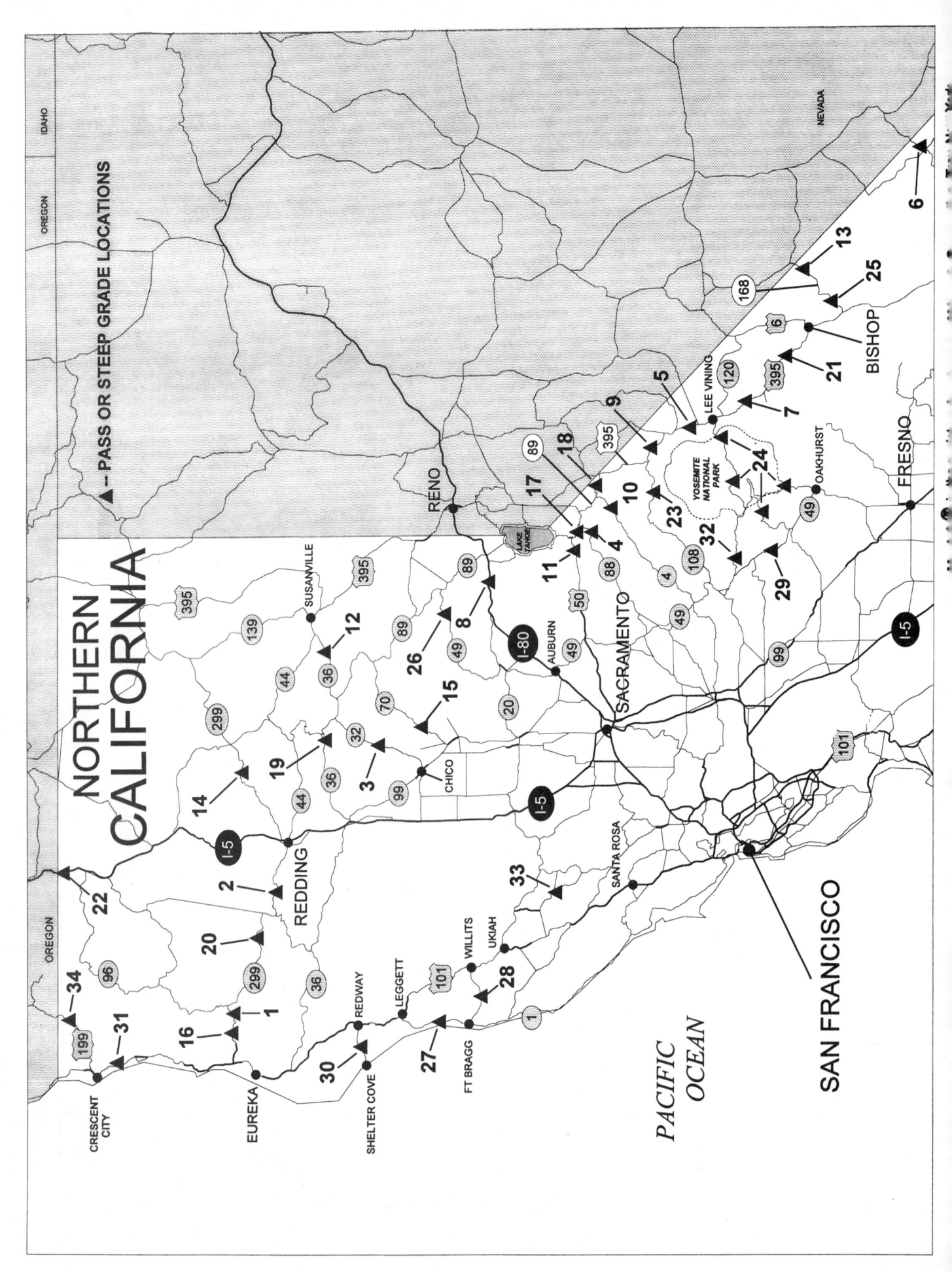

NORTHERN CALIFORNIA

1. BERRY SUMMIT
2. BUCKHORN SUMMIT
3. CALIFORNIA HIGHWAY 32
4. CARSON PASS
5. CONWAY SUMMIT
6. DAYLIGHT PASS *
7. DEADMAN SUMMIT
8. DONNER PASS
9. DEVIL'S GATE SUMMIT
10. EBBETTS PASS
11. ECHO SUMMIT
12. FREDONYER SUMMIT
13. GILBERT SUMMIT *
    (see WESTGARD PASS)
14. HATCHET MOUNTAIN SUMMIT
15. JARBOE PASS
16. LORD ELLIS SUMMIT
17. LUTHER PASS
18. MONITOR PASS
19. MORGAN SUMMIT
    (see FREDONYER SUMMIT)
20. OREGON MOUNTAIN SUMMIT
21. SHERWIN SUMMIT
22. SISKIYOU SUMMIT
23. SONORA PASS
24. TIOGA PASS
25. WESTGARD PASS *
26. YUBA PASS

27 thru 34 see New Info on page 117

* In both Northern California and Southern California directories

1 BERRY SUMMIT elev. 2803'
(on California Highway 299 west of Willow Creek, CA)

This summit is about 11 miles west of Willow Creek. The eastbound descent is **5-6% for about 4 miles** with many 35 mph curves. The grade then eases to 3-4% with more curves and then rolls up and down to Willow Creek.

There is a sign at the summit for westbound traffic--"7% grade next 7 miles." The grade varies during the first 3 miles but **the last 4 miles are steady 7% with 40 mph curves and 40 mph truck speed limit.** When the bottom of the hill is reached, the climb up to Lord Ellis Summit begins.

2 BUCKHORN SUMMIT elev. 3213'
(on California Highway 299 west of Whiskeytown, CA)

This is a heavily traveled road. **"Tractor trailers over 30' in length between kingpin and rear axle not advised."** This warning sign for westbound traffic is posted and ignored east of Buckhorn Summit. If you look at the map of northern California you will see that there are not many roads to choose from if you want to get to the coast. This road is not ideal but State highway 36 to the south is not a good alternative if you are in a large vehicle. If you suffer from motion sickness, State highway 36 is not a good alternative in any vehicle.

The eastbound descent from Buckhorn Summit is about **6% for 5 1/2 miles and then 4% for a couple of miles.** Sharp curves are constant including 20 mph hairpins. The road alternates between 2 lane and 3 lane.

The curves during the westbound descent are not as sharp or constant as on the east side. The grade is about **6% for 2 miles**, then 3 miles of 2-4%, then short sections of steeper grade. A few miles down the road is a **2 mile 6% descent.**

NORTHERN CALIFORNIA

3   CALIFORNIA HIGHWAY 32
(between Chico and California Highway 36/89)
"Tractor-semis over 30' kingpin to rear axle not advised next 29 miles."
This sign appears just after turning onto highway 32 southbound from highway 36/89. It is a very narrow and winding road with many steep grades in both directions. Most of these steep grades are short but some are several miles in length.

4   CARSON PASS elev. 8573'
(on California Highway 88 south of Lake Tahoe, CA)
"Trucks with single drive with two trailers prohibited in snow control area." A sign with this message is posted on State highway 88.

The summit of Carson Pass is about 9 miles west of the junction of State highways 88 and 89. The eastbound descent begins with a sign--**"8% grade next 3 miles--trucks use lower gear."** After about 3 1/2 miles of descent the grade eases for about 3/4 mile and then descends at about **6% for 2 1/4 miles.** At this point the grade eases again for a couple of miles.

About 1/4 mile past the junction of 88 and 89 the grade starts back down and for **9 miles it will vary between 3% and 8%. Most of it is in the 4-6% range. The total descent is about 18 miles.**

The westbound descent from the summit of Carson Pass begins with about **5 miles of 5-6% grade.** The rest of the descent is rolling hills for many miles. Since Carson Pass summit is 8573', and the Sacramento Valley to the west is just above sea level, there will obviously be a lot of descent spread over many miles. Highway 88 is a roller coaster descent and would be too confusing to try to describe. There is almost 20 miles of road between the 8000' mark and the 7000' mark, but there is only 12 miles of road between the 7000' and 5000' marks. Some grades are in the 7% range for a couple of miles.

5   CONWAY SUMMIT elev. 8138'
(on US 395 south of Bridgeport, CA)
Conway Summit is about 13 miles south of Bridgeport. The northbound descent from the summit **starts with about 3 miles of 3-5% grade.** At this point there is a warning sign--**"6% grade next 3 miles."** The road alternates from 2 lane to 3 lane to 4 lane.

The southbound descent begins with a sign--**"6% grade next 4 miles."** After this 4 mile descent the grade eases for almost 2 miles and then begins stairstepping down with short 6% hills with flat sections in between. Twelve miles south of the summit is Lee Vining, California.

NORTHERN CALIFORNIA

6   **DAYLIGHT PASS** elev. 4315'
(on California State Highway 374 just south of the California-Nevada state line in Death Valley National Monument, CA)

Commercial trucking is prohibited in Death Valley National Monument. The northbound descent from the summit of Daylight Pass begins with about 1/2 mile of 6-7% grade with 30 mph curves. The next 2 miles are about 5% followed by 2-3% grade for several miles as you leave the park.

The southbound descent from the summit begins with a sign--**"Steep grade next 13 miles--use lower gear."** Most of this 13 miles is 6-7% grade with some stretches of 7-8% grade. The road is winding with 25, 30, and 45 mph curves. There is a T intersection with a stop sign at the bottom of the hill. This is the junction of State highways 374 and 267. **Use caution on this hill.**

7   **DEADMAN SUMMIT** elev. 8041'
(on US 395 south of Lee Vining, CA)

Deadman Summit is about 15 miles south of Lee Vining on US 395. The descent northbound is very gradual. Most of the grade is 1-3% with a couple of 5-6% sections that are less than a mile in length. The descent continues all the way to Lee Vining.

The southbound descent from the summit begins with a sign--"6% grade next 2 miles." After the 2 miles of descent there is a 1 mile climb at about 5% followed by 7 miles of stairstepping descent with grades that are mostly 2-4%. There are three sections of 5-6% that are less than a mile each.

The road goes from 2 lane to 4 lane during the climb up the north slope with 55 mph speed limit.

IN TRAILER BRAKE CONTROLS...
THERE ARE GOOD BUYS...
—AND—
THERE ARE GOOD BYES...

MARK-4   ACTUATOR   QUANTUM

PENDULUMS   LEVELING   INERTIA

Now is the time to replace your pendulum operated trailer brake control with a new state-of-the-art all electronic trailer brake control from Jordan Research. *No* pendulums, *no* leveling, *no* need for inertia, and *no* constant adjusting.

No other brake control manufacturer gives you as many choices as does Jordan Research. There is a Jordan Electronic Trailer Brake Control for every pocketbook, every dashboard configuration, and every braking requirement. Be it for 2, 4, 6, or 8 brakes, light duty or heavy duty; if it has electric brakes, there is a Jordan control for it!

 *Send for our informative brochure:*
jordan research corporation
6244 Clark Center Avenue • Sarasota, Florida 34238

Dealer Inquiries Invited.
(941) 923-9707

NORTHERN CALIFORNIA

8 DONNER PASS elev. 7239'
(on I-80 west of the California-Nevada state line)

The summit of Donner Pass is about 27 miles west of the California-Nevada state line. The eastbound descent from the summit begins with a sign--**"5 miles downgrade."** The grade is about **5% for 3 miles** and then 2-4% for about 3 1/2 miles. There are some rolling hills and short descents in the 3-5% range over the next 11 or 12 miles. About 18 miles down from the summit is a sign--**"5% grade next 3 miles."**

The westbound descent from the summit of Donner Pass begins with a sign--**"40 miles downgrade."** This downgrade continues past Colfax or to within 14 miles of Auburn, California. There are approximately **33 truck advisory signs** along the descent.

Examples:
"2 miles 5% grade--advise 50 mph"
"Truckers--advise 50 mph--save your brakes--drift low rpm."
"Truckers--let 'er drift--use minimum power--let 'em cool."
"Truckers--upgrade ahead--crank up."
"Truckers--steep downgrade ahead--check your brakes."
"Truckers--upgrade--easy going to Auburn."

There are *two runaway truck ramps.* They are well marked ahead of time. Both exit to the right and the ramps are along the shoulder at the same grade as the road. The first is 25 miles down from the summit and the second is 4 1/2 miles later. There is a 3 mile stretch of 6% as you approach the first escape ramp. Most of the descents are short and they are usually followed by a lesser grade or flat stretch or even upgrade. Even so, brakes can still be overheated on this hill.

There is one inconsistency to be aware of regarding the signs. About 1 mile down from the summit (westbound) there is a sign saying--**"2 miles 5% grade--advise 50 mph."** This is true enough but at the end of the 2 miles there is another sign saying--**"2 miles of 5%--advise 50 mph."** In other words, it is a **4 mile 5% hill**.

9 DEVIL'S GATE SUMMIT elev. 7519'
(on US 395 north of Bridgeport, CA)

Devil's Gate Summit is about 11 1/2 miles north of Bridgeport. The descent on both sides of this summit is fairly gradual. There are very short sections of 3-5% grade followed by lesser grade. The gradual descent continues for many miles north toward Coleville and for about 5 miles to the south toward Bridgeport.

NORTHERN CALIFORNIA

10 EBBETTS PASS elev. 8730'
(on California Highway 4 southwest of Markleeville, CA--includes PACIFIC GRADE SUMMIT)

This pass is subject to winter closures. Between Markleeville and the junction of State highways 4 and 89 there are truck warning signs for westbound traffic--**"Tractor-semis over 36' kingpin to rear axle not advised."** A little farther down the road--**"Tractor-semis over 30' kingpin to rear axle not advised next 55 miles"** and **"Trailers not advisable beyond this point."** Just about 2 miles west of the junction of 4 and 89 is another sign--**"Ebbetts Pass ahead--very steep, narrow, winding road--vehicles over 25' not advisable."** This would, of course, apply to vehicles going over this pass from either direction.

The descent eastbound from the summit back towards Markleeville is about **6 miles of mostly 9-11% grade with 10 mph hairpin turns** and many other sharp curves. There is little room to swing wide during the turns because of vertical rock on the shoulder or drop-offs. The road is so narrow the highway department doesn't even paint a center stripe.

The descent westbound from the summit is similar as far as road conditions. The **first 5 miles west of the summit are mostly 6-10% grade.** Then, after about 1/2 mile of fairly flat grade the climb up to Pacific Grade Summit begins. This climb is about **3 miles of 10-12% grade** with sharp curves and narrow road. Large vehicles should avoid this route.

The descent from the Pacific Grade Summit to the west is a rolling and stairstepping descent for over 50 miles. The road widens and improves about 7 miles down from the summit. There are many sections of 5-7% grade during the descent but they are usually short.

11 ECHO SUMMIT elev. 7382'
(on US 50 west of South Lake Tahoe, CA)

The eastbound descent from Echo Summit is about **4 miles of 5-6% grade** with 30 and 35 mph curves. It is a 2 lane road.

The westbound descent from Echo Summit starts with about 5 miles of grade that stairsteps down the hill. There are sections of 5-6% grade with flat stretches or sections of lesser grade in between. About 5 miles down the hill there is a sign--**"6% grade next 3 miles."** This grade is more steady with sharp curves. About a mile after passing thru Strawberry the grade eases and begins stairstepping down.

About 4 1/2 miles after Strawberry there are signs--**"Truck speed limit 35"** and **"Hill--trucks use lower gear next 4 miles."** The grade varies from 5-7% until reaching Kyburz, California where it eases to about 3-4%. There are **several more miles of 4-6% grade after Kyburz.** The road continues an erratic descent for many miles--all the way past El Dorado Hills.

12 FREDONYER SUMMIT elev. 5748'
(on California Highway 36 west of Susanville, CA)
MORGAN SUMMIT elev. 5750'
(on California Highway 36 between Mineral and Mill Creek, CA)

The westbound descent from Fredonyer Summit is about **2 miles of 6% grade** with 40 mph curves. The eastbound descent is about **3 miles of 6%** with 40 mph curves.

Morgan Summit is farther west on State highway 36. It is between Mineral and Mill Creek. The descent from Morgan Summit is about the same eastbound as it is westbound. Both sides are about **3 1/2 miles of 6% grade** with numerous 35 mph curves.

There is a sign at Mineral for westbound traffic--**"Tractor-semis over 30' kingpin to rear axle not advised next 8 miles."**

13 GILBERT SUMMIT--see WESTGARD PASS

14 HATCHET MT. SUMMIT elev. 4368'
(on California Highway 299 east of Montgomery Creek, CA)

Hatchet Mt. Summit is about 11 miles east of Montgomery Creek. The eastbound descent is a steady **6% for about 3 miles** with 45 and 50 mph curves. Burney, CA is 6 miles east of the summit.

The westbound descent begins with 1/2 mile of 5-6% grade. The next 6 1/2 miles the grade varies from 1% to 6% in rolling hills. The steeper sections are not very long. About 7 miles west of the summit there is a sign--"3 miles of 6 1/2% grade." There is a brake check area for westbound traffic. ***There is a runaway truck ramp 2 1/2 miles down the hill from the brake check area.*** The speed limit is 35 mph. The road alternates between 2 lane and 3 lane. There is about 1/2 mile of 6% grade after the escape ramp and one mile later you enter Montgomery Creek.

15 JARBO PASS elev. 2330'
(on California Highway 70 northeast of Oroville, CA)

The westbound descent from the summit of Jarbo Pass begins with about **2 1/2 miles of 4-6% grade**. The grade eases for about 1/4 mile and then it's back down at about **6% for another 2 1/2 miles**. Again the grade eases for 1/2 mile, then back down at **6% for 3/4 mile**. The grade eases once again for about 1 1/2 miles and then back down again at **6% for 1 1/2 miles**. Most of the descent is 4 lane road.

The eastbound descent starts with a sign saying--**"4% grade next 6 miles."** This is a narrow, winding, 2 lane road with little or no shoulder in some places. About 5 1/2 miles down from the summit the road makes a hard right turn and crosses a bridge high over the Feather River. Use extreme caution in bad weather. If you miss the turn, none of the options are good.

NORTHERN CALIFORNIA

16 LORD ELLIS SUMMIT elev. 2263'
(on California Highway 299 west of Berry Summit and Willow Creek, CA)

The eastbound descent from Lord Ellis Summit is a **steady 6% for about 5 miles.** The westbound descent is also about **5 miles of 6%** but there are a couple of very short sections of 2-4% grade during the descent.

17 LUTHER PASS elev. 7740'
(on California Highway 89 between US 50 and State 88 south of Lake Tahoe, CA)

The summit of Luther Pass is about 8 1/2 miles south of the junction of US 50 and State 89 highways. The northbound descent from the summit starts with almost 2 miles of slight grade. **The next 4 miles are steady 6-7% grade.** The last 2 1/2 miles to the junction with US 50 are fairly flat.

The southbound descent from the summit begins with about **2 miles of 6-7% grade** followed by 1/2 mile of 5%. The grade flattens out just before the junction with State highway 88. Going west at this junction will take you over Carson Pass (see Carson Pass). Going east on State 88 **will include about 9 miles of descent. The grade varies between 3% and 8% with most of it in the 4-6% range.**

18 MONITOR PASS elev. 8314'
(on California Highway 89, between US 395 and State Highway 4, south of Lake Tahoe, CA)

This pass is posted with warnings--"Tractor-semis over 36' kingpin to rear axle not advised."

The eastbound descent from the summit of Monitor Pass begins with about 1 mile of 4-5% grade. At this point there is a sign--**"8% grade next 8 miles." This grade is steady** except for a one mile stretch near the bottom where the grade eases to about 5%. The **last 1/2 mile** to the stop sign at the junction with US 395 **is back to 8%.** There are 25 to 40 mph curves.

The westbound descent begins with a short drop and climb to a second summit about 3/4 mile to the west. There is a brake check area at this point and the **truck speed limit is 20 mph all the way to the bottom of the hill 7 1/2 miles ahead. The grade is mostly in the 7-10% range for the 7 1/2 mile descent.** There are a couple of short sections where the grade eases to about 5%. At the bottom of the hill is a stop sign and T intersection. This is the junction of State highways 89 and 4.

19 MORGAN SUMMIT--see FREDONYER SUMMIT

20 OREGON MOUNTAIN SUMMIT elev. 2888'
(on California Highway 299 west of Weaverville, CA)

According to the warning signs at the top of the hill, the descent is about the same on both sides of Oregon Mountain Summit--**"8% grade next 3 miles."** The eastbound descent continues right to the edge of Weaverville.

The westbound descent has a *runaway truck ramp* **1.3 miles down from the summit.** There are 30 and 35 mph curves before you reach the escape ramp. The ramp is in the middle of a long 30 mph curve to the left. It goes uphill but is very short.

Three miles down from the summit the grade eases to about 4% for 1 mile and then 6% for 1/2 mile and then eases again into Junction City.

NORTHERN CALIFORNIA

21 SHERWIN SUMMIT elev. 7000'
(on US 395 north of Bishop, CA)

The northbound descent from Sherwin Summit is rolling 2-4% grade for about 4 miles.

The southbound descent begins with about 3/4 mile of 3%. At this point there is a sign--**"Brake check area 1/4 mile--trucks use pullout."** The grade gets steeper and almost 2 miles down from the summit is a sign--**"6% grade next 8 miles." The truck speed limit is 35 mph. The grade is steady and may be a little more than 6% for the first 3 1/2 miles. The grade does last the full 8 miles.**

This is a good 4 lane road with few curves. *There are no escape ramps.*

22 SISKIYOU SUMMIT elev. 4310'
(on I-5 just north of the Oregon-California state line)

Chains may be required on this hill in winter. Siskiyou Summit is about milepost 4 1/2 on the Oregon side of the state line. There are *two escape ramps on the north side of the hill.* The descent is *7 miles of 6% on both sides of the hill.*

The northbound descent is a **steady 6% grade with 55 mph truck speed limit** and 50 mph curves. *The first runaway truck ramp is at milepost 6.2 and the second is at milepost 9.4.* They are 1 3/4 and 5 miles down from the summit.

The southbound descent starts down at 6%. About 2 1/4 miles down from the summit the grade eases to about 4% for 1 1/2 miles. It then goes back to 6% for another 1 1/2 miles and then eases again for 1 1/4 miles. Then it's back downhill at 6% for 1 1/2 miles. At this point there is a sign--**"4% grade next 2 miles."** Two miles farther down the hill there is an inspection station--all vehicles must stop. "Brakeless trucks use left lane."

About 4 miles south of the inspection station there is a 1 1/2 mile 6% descent and then a **4 mile 6% climb and then a 3 mile 5% descent.**

There is also a **3 mile 5% southbound descent** that bottoms out at Dunsmuir, California.

23 SONORA PASS elev. 9626'
(on California Highway 108 east of Sonora, CA)

This pass is subject to winter closure. There is a sign for westbound traffic at the junction of US 395 and State 108 that should get the attention of anyone thinking of driving this pass in a large vehicle--**"26% grade 10 miles ahead."** An employee of the California Department of Transportation indicated that this information is correct, although for a very short section of road on the east slope. However, there are **10 to 15% grades** in a number of places on both sides of the pass. The DOT employee also indicated that a number of trucks try the pass every year and cannot successfully negotiate the hairpin turns and must be towed out. The road is very narrow with sharp and steep turns.

The westbound descent from the summit to Kennedy Meadows is about **10 miles of grades that vary from 6% to 14%.** There are a few short stretches where the grade eases or even goes uphill but most of the descent will be very steep downhill grade. West of Kennedy Meadows the grade rolls up and down, usually in short stretches of 6-7%. There is a 2 mile 6% stretch just east of Strawberry and **much of the last 10 miles into Sonora are 6-7%. The last 6 miles into Sonora are steady 6% descent.**

The eastbound descent from the summit is about **10 miles of grade that varies from 7% to 15% plus the short section of 26%.** The road is very narrow and winding with very sharp curves. After reaching the valley floor, the road rolls up and down for 5 miles to the junction of US 395 and State 108.

NORTHERN CALIFORNIA

24 TIOGA PASS elev. 9945'
(on California Highway 120 between Lee Vining and the east entrance to Yosemite Park, CA)

Commercial trucking thru Yosemite National Park is prohibited. This pass is subject to winter closures. At the junction of US 395 and State 120 there is a sign for westbound traffic--**"Steep grades--difficult for trailers"** (referring to the westbound climb).

The summit of Tioga Pass is at the east entrance to Yosemite Park, 12 1/4 miles west of the junction of State 120 and US 395.

The eastbound descent from the park entrance begins with 1/2 mile of 6% grade and then 3-4% grade for about 2 1/2 miles. **The next 5 miles are very steep with grades mostly in the 7-8% range.** After this 5 mile stretch the grade varies from about 5% to almost flat for the next 3 1/2 miles. The last 1/2 mile before the junction with US 395 is about 7% grade. The road on this side of the pass is good 2 lane. For westbound traffic the road gets narrow and rough after entering the park. The initial descent is rolling with short 6% hills.

Trying to describe all the roads in the park would be very confusing because the valley floor is about the only flat spot in the park. Obviously any road leading to the valley floor is going to include some long, steep grades. For instance, if you come into the park over Tioga Pass on 120 there are about **9 miles of 5-6%** after you leave 120 and turn toward Yosemite Valley. This is a narrow and winding road with **three tunnels**. All three tunnels have arched tops. **The vertical clearance *at the curb* is 13' 8" at the first tunnel and 10' 4" at the second and third tunnels.**

Leaving the park on State 140 toward El Portal includes about **7 miles of 6-7% descent**. This is also a narrow and winding road with a couple of places where the rocks hang out over the downhill lane (westbound). There are also long, steep grades both uphill and downhill on State 41 which is the south entrance to the park.

25 WESTGARD PASS elev. 7271' and GILBERT SUMMIT elev. 6374'
(on California Highway 168 east of Big Pine, CA)

As you turn off of US 395 and onto State Highway 168 you will be greeted by a series of warnings about Westgard Pass. The warnings include--**"Tractor-semis over 30' kingpin to rear axle not advised next 36 miles"** and **"Warning--steep grade, sharp curves, narrow pavement ahead--not recommended for large or heavy vehicles."** The summit of Westgard Pass is about 14 miles east of the junction of US 395 and State 168.

The westbound descent from the summit is a roller coaster ride including **6 to 9% grades for about 10 miles**. The road is narrow with 20, 25, 30, and 35 mph curves all the way down. There is a section of **one lane road** thru a cut in the rocks. It is only about 1/4 mile long and is about 3 miles down from the summit. The eastbound descent is about **9% for 1 mile, then 7% for 3 miles, then 6% for 3 miles.** The road is slightly better than the west side with numerous 25 and 35 mph curves.

Gilbert Summit is about 19 miles east of Westgard Pass summit. The westbound descent from Gilbert Summit is about **4 miles of winding 6-9% grade** with 15, 20, and 25 mph curves.

The eastbound descent is **8% for 1 mile, then 5-6% for 2 miles**. It is a winding road with 25 mph curves. The junction with State 266 is 5 miles east of the summit.

NORTHERN CALIFORNIA

26 YUBA PASS elev. 6701'
(on California Highway 49 west of Sattley, CA)

Trucks over 30' kingpin to rear axle not advised. The summit of Yuba Pass is about 7 miles west of Sattley. The eastbound descent to Sattley starts with **5-7% grade for about 6 miles.** There is a 15 mph hairpin turn near the top of the grade and 20 and 25 mph curves most of the way down. The last mile into Sattley is about 3-4% grade.

The first mile of the westbound descent is 6-7% and then the grade is about 5% for 3 miles. The next 4 miles the grade varies from 2-4%. There are 25 mph curves. **At this point the grade steepens to 4-6% and continues thru Sierra City, 4 1/2 miles down the road and then another 4 miles toward Downieville.** The remaining 8 miles to Downieville are less steep but the road is very narrow at times and quite curvy. Going into Downieville there is a one lane bridge and the main street of town is extremely narrow with a 10 mph speed limit.

27 thru 34 see New Info on page 117.

NORTHERN CALIFORNIA

SOUTHERN CALIFORNIA

SOUTHERN CALIFORNIA

1. CAJON PASS
2. CRESTWOOD SUMMIT
   (see LAGUNA SUMMIT)
3. DAYLIGHT PASS *
4. GILBERT SUMMIT *
   (see WESTGARD PASS)
5. GRAPEVINE
6. HALLORAN SUMMIT
   (see MOUNTAIN PASS)
7. IBEX PASS
8. JUBILEE PASS
   (see SALSBERRY PASS)
9. LAGUNA SUMMIT
10. MOUNTAIN PASS
11. MOUNTAIN SPRINGS SUMMIT
    (see SOUTH PASS)
12. MOUNTAIN SPRINGS PASS
    (see LAGUNA SUMMIT)
13. SALSBERRY PASS
14. SOUTH PASS
15. TECATE SUMMIT
    (see LAGUNA SUMMIT)
16. TEHACHAPI SUMMIT
17. TEJON PASS
    (see GRAPEVINE)
18. TOWNE PASS
19. WESTGARD PASS *

20 thru 32 see New Info on pages 117 & 118

* In both Southern California and Northern California directories.

1 CAJON PASS elev. 4190'
(on I-15 south of Victorville, CA)

There is very little descent on the northbound side of Cajon Pass. The southbound descent begins with signs--**"Downgrade next 12 miles--trucks check brakes"** and **"Truck speed limit 45 mph"** and **"Truck scales 5 miles"** and **"6% grade next 4 miles"** and **"Runaway truck ramp 2 1/2 miles."**

The grade may be a bit more than 6% down to the escape ramp where it eases for a very short distance and then goes back to 6% until reaching the truck scales. After the scales the grade eases to about 2-3% for 3 miles, then goes to about **5% for another 4 1/2 miles.**

This road has 4 lanes downhill and a great deal of traffic.

2 CRESTWOOD SUMMIT-- see LAGUNA SUMMIT

3 DAYLIGHT PASS elev. 4315'
(on California Highway 374 just south of the California-Nevada state line in Death Valley National Monument, CA)

Commercial trucking is prohibited in Death Valley National Monument. The northbound descent from the summit of Daylight Pass begins with about 1/2 mile of 6-7% grade with 30 mph curves. The next 2 miles are about 5% followed by 2-3% grade for several miles as you leave the park.

The southbound descent from the summit begins with a sign--**"Steep grade next 13 miles--use lower gear."** Most of this 13 mile descent is 6-7% grade with some stretches of 7-8% grade. The road is winding with 25, 30, and 45 mph curves. There is a T intersection with a stop sign at the bottom of the hill. This is the junction of State highways 374 and 267. *Use caution on this hill.*

SOUTHERN CALIFORNIA

4 **GILBERT SUMMIT**--see WESTGARD PASS

5 **GRAPEVINE HILL** and **TEJON PASS** elev. 4144'
(on I-5 south of Bakersfield between Grapevine and Gorman, CA)

The hill known as "The Grapevine" is actually part of the northbound descent from the summit of Tejon Pass. "The Grapevine" is the last 5 miles of the descent and bottoms out at the town of Grapevine, California. The northbound descent from the summit of Tejon Pass begins with 1 1/2 miles of 5-6% grade, then 1 1/2 miles of 4% grade, and then about 2 miles of 3% grade. At this point there is a section of 5% about 1/4 mile long and then the grade eases for 3/4 mile. **"The Grapevine" is still ahead. The truck speed limit is 35 mph and there are warning signs about the runaway truck ramp and "5 miles 6% downgrade--Trucks use lower gear." The grade is steady 6-7% and the runaway truck ramp is about 3 1/2 miles down. It exits to the right and goes uphill. There are about 2 miles of 6-7% grade after the escape ramp. The total descent from the top of Tejon Pass to the bottom of "The Grapevine" is about 12 miles.**

The southbound descent from the summit of Tejon Pass continues for almost 30 miles to just north of Santa Clarita, California. There is a brake inspection area at the top of the pass.

The descent begins with a **couple of miles of 5-6% grade** and then begins a stairstepping descent with varying grades and lengths for about 18 miles. Most of the grades are either not very steep or not very long. About 20 miles down from the summit there is another brake inspection area and a sign--**"Trucks use lower gear next 5 miles." Truck speed limit is 40 mph**. The grade goes to about 5% for a mile and then eases for a mile. Then there is another warning sign--**"5% grade next 5 miles."** After the 5 miles the grade goes to 3-4% for a mile before easing.

6 **HALLORAN SUMMIT**--see MOUNTAIN PASS

7 **IBEX PASS** elev. 2250'
(on California Highway 127 south of Shoshone, CA)

The southbound descent from the summit of Ibex Pass begins with a sign--**"Steep grade next 7 miles."** The first 3 miles are 5-6% downhill followed by 4 miles of 4% grade with 45 and 50 mph curves. The northbound descent is more gradual with about 7 miles of 2-4% grade.

8 **JUBILEE PASS**--see SALSBERRY PASS

24

9 LAGUNA SUMMIT elev. 4055'
CRESTWOOD SUMMIT elev. 4109'
TECATE SUMMIT elev. 4140'
MOUNTAIN SPRINGS PASS elev. 3241'

(These summits are between El Cajon and Ocotillo, CA on I-8)

Crosswinds can be very strong along this entire stretch of highway--especially on the east side of Mountain Springs Pass.

Laguna Summit is about 1 1/2 miles east of the Pine Valley exit. The westbound descent begins with about 2 1/2 miles of 4-5% downhill before starting a 1 1/4 mile 4-5% climb. After topping this hill the road will make a 3000' drop in elevation spread out over 18 miles.

The grade starts down immediately at about 6%. Soon there is a warning sign--**"6% grade next 13 miles."** This warning is repeated at one mile intervals all the way down the hill. **The grade is fairly steady for about 4 miles near the top and for another 4 miles near the town of Alpine.** In between these two stretches are about 6 miles of stairstepping grade with short, steep sections alternating with short sections of lesser grade.

The eastbound descent from Laguna Summit starts with about **3 miles of 5-6% grade** and then eases before beginning the climb to Crestwood Summit. This climb is about 3-4% for several miles and **the last 4 miles to Crestwood Summit is about 6% uphill grade.**

It is 3 miles between Crestwood Summit and Tecate Summit and the grades are mostly 3-4%.

The eastbound descent from Tecate Summit is about **9 miles of variable grade. It is 4-6%** with some stretches of lesser grade. There is about a 1000' drop in elevation during this stretch before beginning a 4 mile climb of about 3% to the summit of Mountain Springs Pass.

The eastbound descent from the summit of Mountain Springs Pass begins with warning signs-- **"9 miles of 6% grade--All trucks check brakes"** and **"Truck speed limit 35 mph"** and *"Runaway truck ramp 5 miles."* The grade doesn't look steep but it's a **steady 6% for most of the 9 miles.** The grade warnings are repeated every mile and there are several warnings about the escape ramp. The ramp exits to the right and is at the same grade as the road.

There are 50 mph curves and the wind can be severe.

SOUTHERN CALIFORNIA

10 **MOUNTAIN PASS** elev. 4731' and **HALLORAN SUMMIT**
(on I-15 south of California-Nevada state line)

The summit of Mountain Pass is about 16 miles south of the California-Nevada state line on I-15.

The northbound descent from the summit begins with a warning sign--**"6% grade next 10 miles--trucks check brakes."** The grade is somewhat less than 6% at the top and bottom of the 10 mile stretch, but the middle section certainly is in the 6% range. There is a *runaway truck ramp about 5 miles down from the summit.* There are several warning signs before you reach the ramp.

The southbound descent is about 8 miles of grade that varies from 2 to 5%. Most of the 8 miles are 2-4% grade. At the end of this 8 mile stretch the climb to Halloran Summit begins. The climb is about 6 miles of 2-3% grade.

The southbound descent from Halloran Summit begins with about 2 miles of 2-3% grade. At this point there is a sign--**"Steep grade next 17 miles."** The grade increases to about 5% for about a mile, then 3% for a mile, then back to 5% for 1 1/2 miles. This variation continues all the way to Baker, California, 17 miles down from the summit. There are some fairly long stretches of 5-6% grade included--certainly enough to warrant a cautious descent for heavy vehicles.

11 **MOUNTAIN SPRINGS SUMMIT**--see SOUTH PASS

12 **MOUNTAIN SPRINGS PASS**--see LAGUNA SUMMIT

13 **SALSBERRY PASS** elev. 3315' and **JUBILEE PASS** elev. 1280'
(on California Highway 178 west of Shoshone, CA)
Commercial trucking is prohibited in Death Valley National Monument.

The eastbound descent from the summit of Salsberry Pass starts with about **4 miles of 5% grade** and 35 mph curves. The remaining grade is 2-3% and variable for about 7 miles to the junction with State 127.

The westbound descent from the summit starts with warning signs--**"Steep grade next 8 miles."** and **"5% grade 4 miles."** **The grade is closer to 6% for the entire 8 miles** with some 35 mph curves.

At the end of the 8 mile descent, a winding 5% climb to the summit of Jubilee Pass begins. The climb is only about 3/4 mile long with 35 mph curves and a 25 mph curve at the summit.

The westbound descent from the summit of Jubilee Pass is almost **5 miles of 6-7% grade.** In the middle of this 5 mile descent is a **3/4 mile stretch of 7-8% grade.** There is another mile of 3-4% grade at the bottom of the hill.

Instant Power You can FEEL! Improves Acceleration, Hill Climbing & Passing!

GIBSON PERFORMANCE EXHAUST SYSTEMS
Complete Exhaust Systems...from Headers to Stainless Steel tip
TRUCKS and MOTORHOMES! • Lowest Price/Highest Quality
Aluminized & Stainless Bolt-on Kits • 50 State Legal • Lifetime Warranty
GIBSON PERFORMANCE EXHAUST SYSTEMS

714/528-3044 • FREE CATALOG • 800/528-3044

SOUTHERN CALIFORNIA

14 SOUTH PASS elev. 2750' and MOUNTAIN SPRINGS SUMMIT elev. 2770'
(on I-40 west of Needles, CA)

The summit of South Pass is about 8 miles west of the western junction of US 95 and I-40. The eastbound descent from the summit starts with about **2 miles of 5-6% grade** and then goes to about 3% for about 5 miles. The westbound descent from the summit is about **4 1/4 miles of 4% grade**. Soon after leveling out the climb to the top of Mountain Springs Summit begins. This climb is about 5 miles long and gradual most of the way. About half of it is in the 3-5% range and the other half 1-2%.

The westbound descent from Mountain Springs Summit is 2-3% for 7 or 8 miles.

15 TECATE SUMMIT--see LAGUNA SUMMIT

16 TEHACHAPI SUMMIT elev. 4064'
(on California Highway 58 at Tehachapi, CA)

Tehachapi Summit is marked just east of town on State highway 58. It is a 4 lane road. The eastbound descent is gradual and spread out over a long distance.

The westbound descent from where the summit is marked begins with almost 3 miles of nearly flat road. At this point there are warning signs--**"Trucks--steep grade and sharp curves ahead"** and **"Steep grade next 14 miles."** About 1/2 mile after the sign the grade increases to about 4% with 55 mph curves. There is another sign--**"4% grade next 3 miles"** but after 2 miles the grade goes to 5-6% for 1 1/2 miles. The grade then eases and begins to vary for about 8 miles. There are stretches of 4-6% grade 2 miles or less alternating with stretches of nearly flat road and one uphill climb of a mile or so.

The next 10 miles start out with a sign--**"6% grade next 3 miles."** The lower part of this 3 mile stretch may be a bit more than 6%. The grade then begins to stairstep down again for the last 7 miles. There are 5-6% stretches 2 miles or less in length alternating with stretches of lesser grade that are usually very short--1/4 to 1/2 mile in length. The flatter sections are usually too short to allow brakes to cool very much. ***The total descent is almost 22 miles in length. Use caution on this hill.***

17 TEJON PASS--see GRAPEVINE

SOUTHERN CALIFORNIA

18 **TOWNE PASS** elev. 4956'
(on California Highway 190 at western edge of Death Valley National Monument, CA)
Commercial trucking is prohibited in Death Valley National Monument.
　　The section of State highway 190 between Stovepipe Wells and the junction of highways 190 and 136 near Owens Lake is difficult from either direction. There are signs advising motorists to turn off air conditioners to avoid overheating. Both sides of Towne Pass are long and steep and there is an unmarked summit between Panamint Springs and Owens Lake. The eastbound descent from the summit of Towne Pass is a **drop in elevation of almost 5000'** to Stovepipe Wells, which is just above sea level. *Large vehicles should use caution on this road whether climbing or descending.*
　　The eastbound descent begins with a sign--**"6% grade next 3 miles."** Parts of these 3 miles may be more than 6%. The road is winding with 30 mph curves. After the 3 miles is a sign--**"8% grade next 5 miles."** At the end of the 5 miles is another sign--**"6% grade next 5 miles."** So there is a **total of 13 miles of 6-8% grade** followed by several miles of about 3% grade into Stovepipe Wells.
　　The westbound descent starts with signs--**"Steep grade next 9 miles"** and **"9% grade next 6 miles."** **The 9% grade is steady** with 45 mph curves. Near the end of the 9% section is a sign--**"5% grade 2 miles."** The 9% grade continues almost a mile after this sign before the 2 miles of 5% begins.
　　About a mile after reaching the bottom of Towne Pass, you will arrive in Panamint Springs. Just west of town a 17 mile climb begins to an unmarked summit. The **first 11 miles of this climb are 6-7% grade** with 20, 25, and 30 mph curves. The next 6 miles are variable grade from short, almost flat stretches to short 3-5% stretches. **(Of course, if you are traveling east this means a very long descent, most of which is 6-7% grade.)**
　　The westbound descent from this unmarked summit covers about 12 1/2 miles. The grade stairsteps down with stretches of 2-3% and 4-5% and 6-7% alternating with stretches of almost flat road. The grade bottoms out near the junction of highways 190 and 136 near Owens Lake.

19 **WESTGARD PASS** elev. 7271' and **GILBERT SUMMIT** elev. 6374'
(on California Highway 168 east of Big Pine, CA)
　　As you turn off of US 395 and onto State Highway 168 you will be greeted by a series of warnings about Westgard Pass. The warnings include--**"Tractor-semis over 30' kingpin to rear axle not advised next 36 miles"** and **"Warning--steep grade, sharp curves, narrow pavement ahead--not recommended for large or heavy vehicles."** The summit of Westgard Pass is about 14 miles east of the junction of US 395 and State 168.
　　The westbound descent from the summit is a roller coaster ride including **6 to 9% grades for about 10 miles**. The road is narrow with 20, 25, 30, and 35 mph curves all the way down. There is a section of **one lane road** thru a cut in the rocks. It is only about 1/4 mile long and is about 3 miles down from the summit. The eastbound descent is about **9% for 1 mile, then 7% for 3 miles, then 6% for 3 miles**. The road is slightly better than the west side with numerous 25 and 35 mph curves.
　　Gilbert Summit is about 19 miles east of Westgard Pass summit. The westbound descent from Gilbert Summit is about **4 miles of winding 6-9% grade** with 15, 20, and 25 mph curves.
　　The eastbound descent is **8% for 1 mile, then 5-6% for 2 miles**. It is a winding road with 25 mph curves. The junction with State 266 is 5 miles east of the summit.

20 thru **32** see New Info on pages 117 & 118.

CLIMB HILLS WITH MORE POWER... AND CRUISE WITH BETTER ECONOMY.

Most RVers share the same performance problems. Sluggish performance on hills, poor passing power and depressing gas mileage.

A Gear Vendors auxiliary transmission can change all that by providing your RV with up to twice the number of forward gears at the press of a button, just like the big commercial trucks.

POWER

For example, your 3 speed automatic will now have 5 speeds from 1st thru drive plus a 6th gear overdrive. Imagine having power with precisely the right gear for any grade. Stop or slow down on a hill and come easily back up to speed with each gear ratio so closely spaced the engine stays in the power on every shift. No longer are you holding up traffic. In fact, you are able to pass slower traffic and do so more safely with just the right gears for power.

ECONOMY

That's right, the same product that gives you all that extra power, also gives you a .78 to 1 overdrive ratio for improved gas mileage. At 22%, this half gear of overdrive is more suitable for your RV than any other factory ratio available, letting you reduce engine rpm and noise without lugging. These are just some of the reasons you'll want a Gear Vendors UNDER/OVERDRIVE™ even if your transmission already has overdrive built into it.

QUALITY

Our products are manufactured jointly with the Hardy Spicer division of GKN and meet the standards of such customers as Fleetwood Motorhomes, Ford, Volvo, and many other Original Equipment Manufacturers who have purchased more than 1 million of our auxiliary transmissions.

Advanced Mechanical, Hydraulic, and Electronic Engineering when compared to any other product available, Gear Vendors is the only "Original Equipment" auxiliary transmission.

Call toll free 1-800-999-9555 for more information or to arrange an installation at your nearest authorized dealer.

VIDEO FEATURE AND BENEFIT TAPE
1/2 hour VHS only $14.95 ($15.88 in CA)
Includes free 3 day shipping. Call:
1-800-999-9555
Trailer Life magazine says, "A must see... informative, factual and specially written for the RVer.

GEAR VENDORS UNDER/OVERDRIVE™

The "GV" symbol and UNDER/OVERDRIVE are trademarks of Gear Vendors Inc., 1717 N. Magnolia, El Cajon, CA 92020

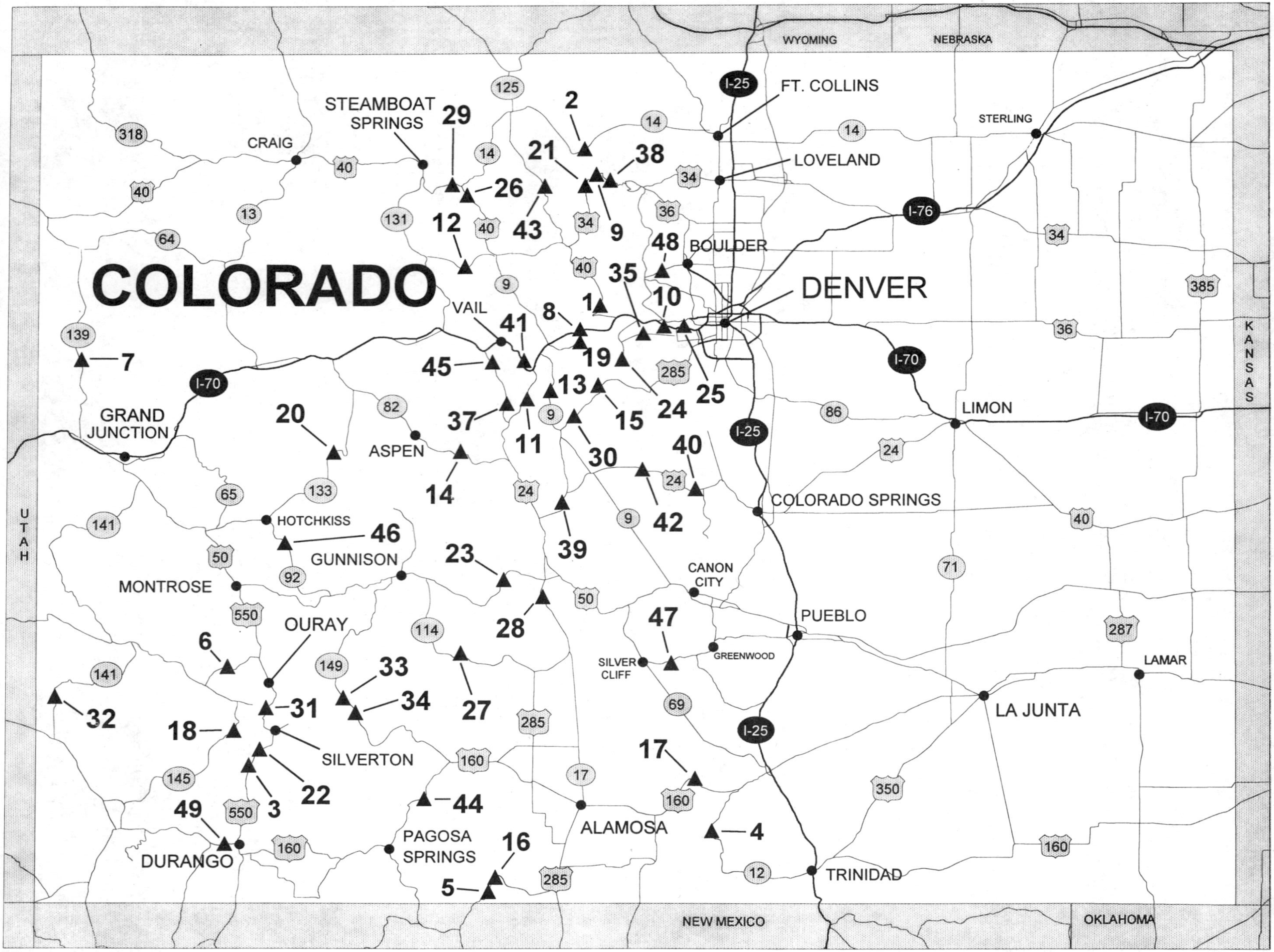

MapInfo® is the registered trademark of MapInfo Corporation, Troy, New York.

COLORADO

1. BERTHOUD PASS
2. CAMERON PASS
3. COALBANK HILL
    (see RED MOUNTAIN PASS)
4. CUCHARAS PASS
5. CUMBRES PASS
6. DALLAS DIVIDE
7. DOUGLAS PASS
8. EISENHOWER TUNNEL
    (also known as STRAIGHT CREEK PASS)
9. FALL RIVER PASS
    (see TRAIL RIDGE HIGH POINT)
10. FLOYD HILL
    (see MT. VERNON CANYON)
11. FREMONT PASS
12. GORE PASS
13. HOOSIER PASS
14. INDEPENDENCE PASS
15. KENOSHA PASS
16. LA MANGA PASS
    (see CUMBRES PASS)
17. LA VETA PASS
18. LIZARD HEAD PASS
19. LOVELAND PASS
20. McCLURE PASS
21. MILNER PASS
    (see TRAIL RIDGE HIGH POINT)
22. MOLAS DIVIDE
    (see RED MOUNTAIN PASS)
23. MONARCH PASS
24. MT. EVANS
25. MT. VERNON CANYON
    (also known as GENESEE HILL)
26. MUDDY PASS
    (see RABBIT EARS PASS)
27. NORTH PASS
28. PONCHA PASS
29. RABBIT EARS PASS
30. RED HILL PASS
31. RED MOUNTAIN PASS
32. SLICK ROCK HILL
33. SLUMGULLION PASS
34. SPRING CREEK PASS
    (see SLUMGULLION PASS)
35. SQUAW PASS
    (see MT. EVANS)
36. STRAIGHT CREEK PASS
    (see EISENHOWER TUNNEL)
37. TENNESSEE PASS
38. TRAIL RIDGE HIGH POINT
39. TROUT CREEK PASS
40. UTE PASS
41. VAIL PASS
42. WILKERSON PASS
    (see UTE PASS)
43. WILLOW CREEK PASS
44. WOLF CREEK PASS
45 thru 49 see New Info on page 118

1 BERTHOUD PASS elev. 11307'
(on US 40 between Empire and Winter Park, CO)

The summit of Berthoud Pass is about 13 miles west of Empire, Colorado. The eastbound descent from the summit starts with about **6 miles of 6% grade** with 20 and 25 mph hairpin turns and 30 and 35 mph curves. Part of the road is 2 lane and part is 3 lane. After passing thru Berthoud Falls there are some rolling hills for 2 or 3 miles and then a **4-5% grade for about 4 miles** to Empire.

The westbound descent is also about **6 miles of 6% grade** with 20 and 25 mph hairpin turns and 25, 30, and 35 mph curves. The descent continues after the 6 miles of 6% but at a lesser grade and the speed limit increases to 55 mph.

COLORADO

2 **CAMERON PASS** elev. 10276'
(on Colorado Highway 14 east of Gould, CO)
The summit of Cameron Pass is about 10 miles east of Gould. The eastbound descent is rolling hills for about 3 miles. At this point there is a truck warning sign-**"steep grade next 10 miles"** but the sign gives no details. It is a rolling descent with some steep sections but they are not very long.

The westbound descent is about **4 miles of 6% grade** with 30 and 35 mph curves.

3 **COAL BANK HILL**--see RED MOUNTAIN PASS

4 **CUCHARAS PASS** elev. 9941'
(on Colorado Highway 12 south of Cuchara, CO)
The summit of Cucharas Pass is near milepost 22 on 12 highway about 5 miles south of Cuchara. The northbound descent from the summit starts with about **4 miles of steady 6% grade.** The road is winding with constant 20, 25, and 30 mph curves. There are scattered short 5-6% hills to Cuchara and beyond with 2-4% grade in between.

The southbound descent is quite different. **The first 1/2 mile is 6-7% followed by about 1/2 mile of 10% (approx.) then another 3/4 mile of 6%. There is a short uphill stretch followed by a mile of 6-10% grade downhill, another short uphill section and back downhill for 2 1/2 miles of 4-6%.** The next 9 miles to Stonewall are up and down in short, steep sections or flat alongside two lakes. There are 20, 25, 35, and 40 mph curves from the summit to Stonewall but it is not as winding as the north side of the pass.

5 **CUMBRES PASS** elev. 10022'
LA MANGA PASS elev. 10230'
(Both of these passes are on Colorado Highway 17 between Antonito, CO and Chama, NM.)
The summit of La Manga Pass is about 28 miles south of Antonito (west as the crow flies). The descent towards Antonito begins with about a mile of 4% grade. At this point there is a sign-**"7% grade next 4 miles"** and **"trucks use lower gear."** The grade is **steady 7%** except for one very short break in the middle that only lasts about 1/4 mile. It is a winding road with 25, 30, and 35 mph curves.

The southbound descent stairsteps down for about 3 miles with short 4-6% grades and then eases up to the summit of Cumbres Pass.

The southbound descent from the summit of Cumbres Pass is spread out over about 9 miles. The **first mile of descent is about 7%** followed by about 1 1/2 miles of 3-4% grade. The next **6 1/2 miles are mostly 6%** with several short sections of 4% scattered along the descent. It is good 2 lane road with 30 and 40 mph curves.

SCRATCH HERE
IF YOU *DON'T* SMELL BURNING BRAKES YOU MUST OWN A

MOUNTAIN TAMER
VARIABLE ENGINE BRAKING
GAS $_{AND}$ DIESEL
Also High Performance Torque Converters

DECEL-O-MATIC CORP
SEE AD ON PAGE 3

6 DALLAS DIVIDE elev. 8970'
(on Colorado Highway 62 west of Ridgeway, CO)

Dallas Divide is about half way between Ridgeway and Placerville, Colorado on state highway 62. Going east from the summit the grade is about **6% for 6 miles.** There are 45 mph curves and the road alternates from 2 lane to 3 lane. The Colorado Dept. of Highways lists Dallas Divide at 6.4% grade on the east side and 5% on the west side.

The westbound descent begins with some rolling hills for about 3 miles then a **5% downhill for about 3 miles.** The road is 2 lane with 45 mph curves. There are rolling hills to the junction of 62 and 145 highways at Placerville.

7 DOUGLAS PASS elev. 8268'
(on Colorado Highway 139 north of Grand Junction, CO)

The summit of Douglas Pass is about 38 miles south of Rangely, Colorado and about 35 miles north of I-70. The summit is about milepost 35. The northbound descent from the summit is about **3 miles of steady 7-8% grade** with 20, 25, and 30 mph curves.

The southbound descent from the summit is almost **6 miles of 6-8% grade** with 25 mph speed limit and **numerous 15 mph curves and switchbacks.** About 2 1/2 miles down from the summit there is a **1/10 mile section of 10 or 12% grade.** After the 6 miles of 6-8% there are several miles of 4% grade.

8 EISENHOWER TUNNEL elev. 11013' (also known as STRAIGHT CREEK PASS)
(at milepost 215 on I-70 west of Georgetown, CO)

Eisenhower Memorial Tunnel is at the summit of Straight Creek Pass. *The tunnel is prohibited to vehicles over 13' 6" in height and Hazardous Material loads that require a placard. These vehicles must go over Loveland Pass on US 6. If Loveland Pass is closed due to bad weather or avalanche, Hazardous Material loads can be routed thru the tunnel one at a time, on the hour every hour, with no other traffic. Over height loads cannot go thru the tunnel at any time. Over width loads should check with tunnel personnel before entering tunnel. There may be work crews in the tunnel with a lane closed.*

When you come out of the tunnel going westbound there are warning signs--**"7% grade next 6 miles--trucks over 30,000 lbs. 30 mph."** The **7% grade is steady for 6 miles** as promised, but that is not the end of the hill. There are about **2 1/2 miles of 5-6% after the 6 miles of 7%.** The hill bottoms out about milepost 205 1/2. There are *two escape ramps* on the west side of Eisenhower. **The first is at milepost 212 and the second is at milepost 209.** Both of these exit to the right and are upsloping ramps. There are several advisory signs as you approach the ramps.

If you are going eastbound and cannot use the tunnel because of height, width, or hazardous cargo you must use Loveland Pass on US 6. Eastbounders who must use Loveland Pass should be aware that the descent on the east side of Loveland comes out just below the Eisenhower Tunnel on I-70. This means about **5 miles of 6% grade** *to descend on Loveland and* **12 miles of 5-6% grade** *on I-70 for a* **total descent of about 17 miles at 5-6%.**

The eastbound descent from Eisenhower Tunnel begins with a sign saying--**"5-6% grade next 12 miles."** Speed limit for trucks over 75,000 lbs. is 32 mph. There are a few breaks in the grade but the majority of the 12 mile descent is in the 5-6% range. The grade continues past Georgetown. The steep part of the descent is over at milepost 228 and a lesser grade continues for several more miles.

COLORADO

9 FALL RIVER PASS--see TRAIL RIDGE HIGH POINT

10 FLOYD HILL--see MT. VERNON CANYON

11 FREMONT PASS elev. 11318'
(on Colorado Highway 91 north of Leadville, CO)

The summit of Fremont Pass is about 12 miles north of Leadville, near Climax, Colorado. The southbound descent from the summit is about **4 1/2 miles of 5-6% grade**. There is a section in the middle of this descent where the grade eases somewhat. There are 40 and 45 mph curves and the road is 3 lane during the steeper sections.

The descent going north from the summit begins with rolling hills. About 2 1/4 miles from the summit is a warning sign--**"Steep grade."** The descent is about **4% for 1 1/2 miles** where there is another sign--**"7% grade next 3 miles."** After the 3 miles of 7% there is another **2 to 3 miles of 5-6%** until the junction with I-70 is reached.

12 GORE PASS elev. 9527'
(on Colorado Highway 134 east of Toponas, CO)

Gore Pass summit is about 11 miles west of the junction of US 40 and Colorado 134. The Colorado Dept. of Highways lists Gore Pass at 6.3% grade.

The westbound descent from the summit starts with about 1 1/2 miles of 6% grade with 20 mph switchbacks and 25 mph curves. Then there is 1/2 mile of uphill followed by another mile of 5-6% curvy downhill. After that are rolling hills.

The eastbound descent from the summit begins with a gradual increase in grade to about 6% and many curves that aren't marked with speed limit signs. About 2 3/4 miles from the summit the road begins rolling up and down for almost 2 miles. At this point there is a truck warning sign--**"Trucks use lower gear"**--and the next **2 1/2 miles are 5-6% grade** with 35 mph curves. The grade eases and begins to roll for a few miles.

13 HOOSIER PASS elev. 11541'
(on Colorado Highway 9 between Breckenridge and Alma, CO)

The Colorado Dept of Highways lists Hoosier Pass at 8% grade on the north side. This descent to the north is indeed steep and it is about 4 miles in length. There are 10, 15, and 20 mph hairpin turns all the way down. The southbound descent is about **3 1/2 miles of curvy 6% grade** and then about 1 1/2 miles of 3-4% grade until reaching Alma.

34

COLORADO

14 INDEPENDENCE PASS elev. 12095'
(on Colorado Highway 82 east of Aspen, CO)

This pass is closed in winter. Vehicles over 35' are prohibited. *On the west side of this pass there are 15 mph hairpin turns that are much less than 2 lanes wide. There is little room to negotiate these turns because of vertical rock walls on one side and vertical drop offs on the other. There is also very little visibility ahead to see if someone is coming from the opposite direction.* **This is certainly a spectacular pass to travel but not in a large vehicle.**

The descent westbound begins with a sign that says--**"Steep grade next 6 miles."** There are sharp curves, including **15 mph hairpin turns** but this upper part is much better road than farther down. The grade is about 6%. About 10 miles down from the summit the road narrows and the next 5 miles are steep and winding with the narrow hairpins described above. The Colorado Dept. of Highways lists this pass at 6%.

The eastbound descent begins with a sign--**"Steep grade next 5 miles--sharp curves."** There are 25 mph curves and **10 mph hairpins** and **parts of the grade during the first 4 1/2 miles seem much steeper than 6%.** After the first 4 1/2 miles the speed limit increases but the grade remains about **5-6% for another 5 to 6 miles**, finally leveling off about 15 miles down from the summit.

15 KENOSHA PASS elev. 10001'
(on US 285 north of Fairplay, CO)

The southbound descent from the summit of Kenosha Pass is only about **2 miles of 6% grade** with 50 mph speed limit. The northbound descent starts with some rolling hills for the first 2 miles with 5-6% downgrade and 55 mph speed limit. **The next 3 miles are more steady descent at 5-6%** followed by 3 more miles of lesser grade.

16 LA MANGA PASS--see CUMBRES PASS

17 LA VETA PASS elev. 9413' (also known as **North La Veta Pass**)
(on US 160 Highway between Fort Garland and Walsenburg, CO)

The summit of La Veta Pass is near milepost 279 about midway between Fort Garland and Walsenburg. The westbound descent from the summit is mostly **3 and 4% grades for 7 or 8 miles** with a couple of short sections of 5-6% grade near the top.

The eastbound descent from the summit begins with a sign that says-**"6% grade next 4 miles."** The grade is fairly **steady 6% for 4 miles followed by 1/2 mile of 3% and then another mile of 6% and then several more miles of 3%.**

35

COLORADO

18 **LIZARD HEAD PASS** elev. 10222'
(on Colorado Highway 145 south of Telluride, CO)

The summit of Lizard Head Pass is about 12 miles south of Telluride, Colorado. The northbound descent is listed by the Colorado Dept. of Highways at 4.1% but seems steeper. The first 3 miles include 35 mph curves on 2 lane road and what seems to be a 5-6% grade. Then there are about 6 miles of rolling hills with 30 and 35 mph curves. **The last 3 miles into Telluride are steady 5-6% downhill** with more 30 mph curves.

If you are going north from Telluride toward Placerville, you will descend from Telluride at about **6-7% for about 3 miles** and then several miles of lesser grade.

The southbound descent from Lizard Head Pass begins with a gentle decline for the first mile and a half. Then the grade steepens to **4-6% for the next 7 miles** with 30 to 40 mph curves.

19 **LOVELAND PASS** elev. 11990'
(on US 6 between Dillon, CO and exit 216 on I-70)

Loveland Pass is the alternate route for vehicles that are not allowed to use Eisenhower Tunnel on I-70. This includes vehicles over 13' 6" in height and any Hazardous Materials load that requires a placard. If Loveland Pass is closed due to avalanche or bad weather, Hazardous Material loads can be routed thru the tunnel one at a time, on the hour every hour, with no other traffic. Over width loads should check with tunnel personnel before entering tunnel. There may be work crews in the tunnel with a lane closed.

The Colorado Dept. of Highways lists Loveland Pass at 6% grade. The westbound descent from the summit of Loveland begins with a sign--**"Trucks stay in lower gear--steep grade next 8 miles." The grade is steady the entire 8 miles** with 20, 25, 30, and 35 mph curves all the way down. The sharper turns are near the top.

The eastbound descent is almost **5 miles of 6% grade** with 20, 25, and 30 mph curves. Eastbound US 6 ties in with I-70 eastbound just east of the Eisenhower Tunnel. **The 12 mile 5-6% descent on I-70 would be in addition to the 5 miles of 6% already descended on US 6.**

20 **McCLURE PASS** elev. 8755'
(on Colorado Highway 133 south of Carbondale, CO)

McClure Pass is steep but not too long on either side. The Colorado Dept. of Highways lists it at **8% grade**. It is a 2 lane road. From the summit the southbound descent is about **3 1/2 miles of 7-8% grade** with 20 to 40 mph curves. After the first 3 1/2 miles the road rolls up and down for 15 miles or more. There are some fairly steep hills along this stretch, some of them lasting 2 or 3 miles.

The northbound descent begins with a truck warning sign--**"Trucks use lower gear next 5 miles."** The descent is steep and curvy. The first **4 miles are about 7-8%** with 30 and 35 mph curves. The road then begins to roll up and down but is still winding with 35 mph curves.

21 **MILNER PASS**--see TRAIL RIDGE HIGH POINT

MOUNTAIN TAMER — *VARIABLE ENGINE BRAKING* GAS ᴬᴺᴅ DIESEL **SEE AD ON PAGE 3**

36

COLORADO

22 MOLAS DIVIDE--see RED MOUNTAIN PASS

23 MONARCH PASS elev. 11312'
(on US 50 west of Salida, CO)

The summit of Monarch Pass is about 22 miles west of Salida and about 17 miles west of Poncha Springs, Colorado. The westbound descent from the summit begins with a truck warning sign that says--**"6% grade next 9 miles."** The Colorado Dept. of Highways lists it at **6.4%**. **The grade is fairly steady** and there are numerous 30, 35, and 45 mph curves during the first 6 miles of the descent. After the 9 miles of 6% grade there are several miles of lesser grade. The town of Sargents, Colorado is about 10 miles west of the summit and there is another 3 miles of downhill after Sargents although the grade is not as steep. *There are no escape ramps going west.*

The descent going east from the summit of Monarch Pass begins with a truck warning sign--**"6% next 10 miles."** There are many 30, 35, and 45 mph curves and the road alternates from 2 lane to 3 lane. *There is a runaway truck ramp 4.8 miles down from the summit.* There are several warning signs before you reach the ramp. There are approximately *5 1/2 miles of 6% grade left after passing the escape ramp and trucks are warned to stay in low gear.* The grade begins to flatten out about 11 miles down from the summit and the remaining 6 miles into Poncha Springs is rolling or gradual descent.

24 MT. EVANS elev. 14264' and SQUAW PASS elev. 9807'
(south of Idaho Springs, CO on Colorado Highways 103 and 5)

The climb to Mt. Evans from Idaho Springs starts a few miles south of town on Colorado 103. A sign warns of **"Steep grades and sharp curves next 7 miles." The climb is 6+%** with continuous 25 mph or less curves on 2 lane road. After 7 miles the junction with State 5 is reached at Echo Lake. The elevation at Idaho Springs is 7540' and Echo Lake is 10650' for a 3110' difference.

From the junction at Echo Lake it is **9 miles of 5-9% grade to Summit Lake and 5 more miles of 10-15% grade to the top of Mt. Evans.** These are the grades listed by the Colorado Dept. of Highways. The road is narrow and rough and in some places there is very little shoulder.

Of course this means a very long and steep descent for any heavy vehicle. From the top of Mt. Evans to Echo Lake would be 14 miles of 5-15% grade and then an additional 7 miles of 6+% grade if the vehicle was going back to Idaho Springs.

Going east from Echo Lake on Colorado 103 should take us over Squaw Pass. Well folks, on the day we drove these roads we found Juniper Pass but not Squaw Pass. We're sure it was there--we just missed it. What we found was as follows: At the junction of 103 and 5 (heading east on 103) there was a sign that said--"Squaw Pass Summit 9 miles." The elevation at the junction is 10650' and we were going uphill. Two miles later we saw a sign for Juniper Pass. Three tenths of a mile later was a sign saying "11000' elevation" and we were still going up. Squaw Pass summit is 9807'. We kept going up for 7/10 of a mile and then started down. This meant we would be going down for about 6 miles before getting to the summit of Squaw Pass. Actually, we went downhill for about **14 miles** and never saw Squaw Pass--it was missing on that day. Nevertheless, the eastbound **descent varies from 4-6% grade** with almost constant 15 to 35 mph curves. It is all fairly good 2 lane road.

From the highest elevation on this road (which was not marked as the summit of anything) going westbound toward Idaho Springs, the descent is fairly **steady 5-6% for about 10 miles** with almost continuous 25, 30, and 35 mph curves.

COLORADO

25 MT. VERNON CANYON (also known as Genesse Hill elev. 7730')
(on I-70 west of Denver, CO)
FLOYD HILL
(on I-70 west of Denver, CO)

The eastbound descent into Mt. Vernon Canyon (also known as Genesee Hill) begins about milepost 253 1/2 on I-70. The truck warning signs read--**"Steep grade--sharp curves next 5 miles--use lower gear"** and **"Vehicles over 30,000 lbs must use right lane"** and **"Vehicles over 30,000 lbs--35 mph."** The grade starts down at about 6% for 1/2 mile and then levels out for a short distance. Another warning sign says--**"Truckers don't be fooled--4 more miles of steep grade and sharp curves"** and **"6% grade--trucks use lower gear next 4 miles."**

There are more warning signs during the descent including advisories about the *runaway truck ramp at milepost 256 1/2.* The escape ramp is where the right shoulder would normally be and is at the same grade as the road. It is 1/2 mile long with a gravel bed and water barrels at the end. **The grade continues for almost 3 miles after the escape ramp.**

Floyd Hill is a westbound descent that begins about milepost 246 1/2 on I-70. It is a **2 mile 6% grade** with 50 and 55 mph curves. At the bottom of the hill is a curving bridge that seems rather narrow by interstate standards.

26 MUDDY PASS--see RABBIT EARS PASS

27 NORTH PASS elev. 10149' (also known as NORTH COCHETOPA PASS)
(on Colorado Highway 114 west of Saguache, CO)

The summit of North Pass is about 30 miles west of Saguache. Highway 114 is a little rough and not too wide. It is 2 lane.

From the summit the descent going east is fairly steep and curvy. The sign at the top of the pass says--**"6% next 3 miles."** There are 45 mph curves during the first mile of descent and then the speed limit goes to 55 mph with a 6% grade. The grade flattens out about 5 1/2 miles down from the summit.

The westbound descent begins with a sign that says--**"7% grade next 2 miles."** It is a 2 lane road with 35 and 45 mph curves. About 2 miles down from the summit the grade eases to **5-6% for the next 2 1/2 miles** and then changes to rolling hills.

28 PONCHA PASS elev. 9010'
(on US 285 south of Poncha Springs, CO)

The descent headed north from the summit of Poncha Pass starts with what seems to be about a **5% grade for 2 miles.** The Colorado Dept. of Highways lists it at 3%. There are fairly constant 45 mph curves. It is a 3 lane road with a passing lane for uphill traffic. The **next 5 miles seem to be about 4%** grade with numerous 45 mph curves. It is a fairly steady descent. The grade levels out about the time the junction with US highway 50 is reached after a **total descent of 7.2 miles**. The town of Poncha Springs is at this junction. Poncha Springs' elevation is 7469' so the drop in elevation from the summit is 1541' in 7.2 miles. There isn't much to tell about the southbound descent from the summit of Poncha Pass. It is 2 lane with a mild grade for a mile or so and then becomes rolling hills. Villa Grove (elev. 7980') is 20 miles south of the summit so it is only a 1030' drop in elevation spread over 20 miles.

29 RABBIT EARS PASS elev. 9426'
(on U.S. 40 east of Steamboat Springs, CO)
MUDDY PASS elev. 8772'
(on U.S. 40 east of Rabbit Ears Pass)

Rabbit Ears Pass has an east summit and a west summit. Between the two summits are rolling hills and the road changes back and forth from 2-lane to 3-lane.

The eastbound descent from Rabbit Ears East summit is about **3 miles of 6% grade** with 30 and 40 mph curves. The grade eases near the junction of U.S. 40 and State 14 highways which is also the summit of Muddy Pass. If you continue east on U.S. 40 the descent down Muddy Pass is only about **2 miles of 5-6% grade.** If you turn east on 14 the descent is short.

The westbound descent from Rabbit Ears West summit begins with a brake check area and warning signs-**"Runaway truck ramp 5 miles ahead"** and **"Trucks use lower gear-7% grade next 7 miles."** *The escape ramp is actually 4 miles down, near milepost 142.*

The grade is very steady at 7% with 45 mph curves. The escape ramp exits to the right and goes uphill. There are *3 miles of 7% grade after the escape ramp. This is a dangerous hill for large or heavy vehicles.*

30 RED HILL PASS elev. 9993'
(on US 285 north of Fairplay, CO)

Red Hill Pass is about 1 mile of 6% grade on each side of the summit.

COLORADO

31 RED MOUNTAIN PASS elev. 11018'
(between Ouray and Silverton, CO on US 550)
MOLAS DIVIDE elev. 10910'
(south of Silverton, CO on US 550)
COAL BANK HILL
(south of Silverton, CO on US 550)

Red Mountain Pass is between Ouray and Silverton on US 550. *It is not a designated truck route and if you have driven it you will understand why. Truckers should go into Ouray from the north and Silverton from the south.* Motorhome and RV drivers may want to take this road but should be advised to use caution. The northbound descent from Red Mountain Pass into Ouray has numerous sharp curves, steep grade, and in many places almost no shoulder at all before the edge of the mountain. To go south from Ouray to Durango one must go over Red Mountain Pass, Molas Divide, and Coal Bank Hill and then the final descents into Durango.

The northbound descent from the summit of Red Mountain Pass toward Ouray is listed by the Colorado Dept. of Highways at 7% and more. The descent begins with a 25 mph speed limit. During the first 3 1/2 miles there are at least ten hairpin turns with speed limits of 10 and 15 mph. The speed limit then goes to 40 mph with curves and then to 55 mph with curves. The grade eases and you think the hill is over but it's not. After about 2 1/2 miles of lesser grade there is a truck warning sign and the speed limit goes back to 25 mph. The next 5 1/2 miles are back to about 7% grade with constant 10, 15, and 20 mph hairpin turns. *There are two tunnels--one is marked at 13' 9" vertical height.* **There is very little shoulder in places. Some of the hairpins are very tight and there is no room to swing wide because of vertical rock walls or vertical dropoffs. The grade and hairpin turns continue all the way into Ouray, 12 1/2 miles down from the summit.**

The southbound descent from the summit of Red Mountain begins with 25 mph curves and steep grade. After about 2 miles the grade gets even steeper to about **6-7% with 20 mph hairpin turns.** This grade lasts about **2 1/4 miles** and then eases somewhat for about 1 1/2 miles and then goes right back to **6-7% for another 2 to 3 miles**. The town of Silverton is entered about 9 1/2 miles down from the summit of Red Mountain Pass.

After leaving Silverton the climb to the summit of Molas Divide begins with about **4 1/2 miles of 7% uphill grade** and 20, 25, and 30 mph curves. The grade then begins a rolling climb for almost 2 miles to the summit of Molas Divide. The southbound descent from the summit is about **4 1/2 miles of steep grade--Colorado Dept. of Highways lists Molas Divide at 7% and more.** After the grade bottoms out the climb to the top of Coal Bank Hill begins.

The climb is about **2 1/4 miles of 6-7% grade** with 25, 30, and 35 mph curves. The southbound descent from the top of Coal Bank Hill begins with a truck warning sign--**"Steep grade next 6 miles." The grade is about 7%** with 25 and 30 mph curves. *There is a runaway truck ramp about 4 1/4 miles down from the top of the hill.* The grade continues at about 7% for almost 2 miles past the escape ramp.

About 6 miles down from the summit the grade eases for about 5 miles and then begins the descent into Durango. There is a truck warning sign--**"Steep grade"** but the sign gives no details. The grade is **5-7% for about 9 miles** but it is not constant. There are several places where the grade eases for 1/2 mile or so and then goes back down at 5-7%.

Heavy vehicles should use caution on all parts of this road.

32 SLICK ROCK HILL
(on Colorado Highway 141 between Slick Rock and Egnar, CO)

Slick Rock Hill is a descent for northbound traffic that begins about milepost 15 or about 5 miles north of Egnar. The descent begins with about 1 mile of 4% grade then 1 mile of 5-6% grade. At this point there are several warning signs-**"Trucks use lower gear-7% grade next 5 miles"** and ***"Runaway truck ramp 2 miles."*** The road is winding with 25 and 30 mph curves and steady grade.

The runaway truck ramp is about milepost 18 1/2. A vehicle must negotiate a 25 or 30 mph curve to the right before getting to the escape ramp. The road then curves left and the escape ramp goes straight ahead and downhill. There are **3 miles of 7% grade after the escape ramp.**

33 SLUMGULLION PASS elev. 11530'
SPRING CREEK PASS elev. 10898'
(Both of these passes are on Colorado Highway 149 south of Lake City, CO)

The summit of Slumgullion Pass is about 9 miles south of Lake City. The Colorado Dept. of Highways lists the grade at **9.4% on the north side and 7.9% on the south side** of this pass. It is all good 2 lane road. Truck warning signs do not indicate the length or percentage of grade.

Starting from the summit and heading north **the descent is steep and steady.** There are 20 and 25 mph curves all the way down and at least one 15 mph hairpin turn. After about **7 1/2 miles of 9%** grade the road levels out and a short hill is climbed before descending the last hill into Lake City.

The summit of Slumgullion Pass is at 11530' and Lake City is at 8671' for a drop in elevation of 2859' in only 9.6 miles. *This is a very long descent for heavy vehicles and it will require brakes in good repair and adjustment and caution on the part of the driver. There are no runaway truck ramps.*

The southbound descent from the summit of Slumgullion Pass starts out around 6% with 20 and 35 mph curves. About 2 miles down from the summit there is a truck warning sign but it does not give length or % of grade. The descent becomes steeper at this point with more 20 and 30 mph curves ahead. **The grade is 7-8% for about 3 miles for a total descent of about 5 miles of 6-8%.**

At this point the climb to the summit of Spring Creek Pass begins. It is only 2 miles away. It is a 6-7% grade with 30 mph curves. Going south from the summit of Spring Creek Pass the speed limit is 55 mph with a fairly gentle grade for 1 1/2 miles. It then gets a little steeper for about 1 1/2 miles. Then it flattens out for 3/4 mile and then back down at 6-7%. The descent continues this roller coaster immitation with varying degrees of steepness (gradually less) to the valley floor, about 12 miles from the summit.

34 SPRING CREEK PASS--see SLUMGULLION PASS

35 SQUAW PASS--see MT. EVANS

36 STRAIGHT CREEK PASS--see EISENHOWER TUNNEL

COLORADO

37 TENNESSEE PASS elev. 10424'
(on US 24 west of Leadville, CO)

The summit of Tennessee Pass is about 8 1/2 miles west of Leadville on US 24. The eastbound descent toward Leadville is only about **1 1/2 miles of 5-6% grade.**

The westbound descent starts with a 20 mph curve and **5-6% grade for about 2 miles.** The grade eases for about 1/2 mile and then goes back to about **6% for almost 3 miles.** The grade then flattens out over a fairly short distance.

38 TRAIL RIDGE HIGH POINT elev. 12183'
FALL RIVER PASS elev. 11796'
MILNER PASS elev. 10759'
(All three of these passes are on US 34 highway in Rocky Mountain National Park, CO)

This road is closed in winter. Commercial truck traffic is prohibited in the park.

The eastbound descent from Trail Ridge High Point is about 15 miles long. **The first 11 miles are 6-7% downhill with 15 and 20 mph curves.** The next 3/4 mile rolls up and down and then the grade is **back down at 5-6% for another 3 miles.**

The westbound descent includes Fall River Pass and Milner Pass. Going west from Trail Ridge High Point the first **1 1/2 miles are 6-7% downhill** with 15 and 20 mph curves. The **next 1 1/2 miles are 5-6% uphill** with 20 mph curves. From this point the **next 12 1/2 miles are downhill at about 6%** with many curves and 15 mph hairpin turns. During these 12 1/2 miles of descent you will pass the Alpine Visitors Center and Fall River Pass summit and Milner Pass summit.

This is a long and steep descent in either direction for large or heavy vehicles. Use caution and be sure equipment is in good order.

39 TROUT CREEK PASS elev. 9346'
(on US 285/24 south of Fairplay, CO)

The summit of Trout Creek Pass is about 22 miles south of Fairplay and about 1 mile south of the junction of US 285 and US 24. The northbound descent is only about 2 or 3 miles long and not too steep. The southbound descent starts with about **4 miles of 5%** and then eases for a mile or so with 45 mph curves. There are several miles of lesser grade until just before Johnson Village. The last 1 1/2 mile or so into Johnson Village is 5-6% grade.

COLORADO

40 UTE PASS elev. 9165'
(on US 24 west of Colorado Springs, CO)
WILKERSON PASS elev. 9507'
(on US 24 west of Lake George, CO)

Ute Pass summit is on the western edge of the town of Divide, Colorado about 21 miles west of Manitou Springs, Colorado (a suburb of Colorado Springs).

The eastbound descent from the summit is either rolling hills or fairly gradual grade most of the 21 miles to Manitou Springs. The 2 lane descent going east starts with almost 6 miles of rolling hills followed by a steady descent of **5-6% lasting about 4 1/2 miles** including right thru the town of Woodland Park. The next 2 miles are rolling again followed by about 8 1/2 miles of fairly steady descent into Manitou Springs. From Woodland Park to Manitou Springs is all 4 lane with 30 and 35 mph curves.

The westbound descent from the summit of Ute Pass is not very steep and it bottoms out around Lake George. It is all 2 lane with 35, 40, and 45 mph curves.

Continuing west from Lake George begins the climb to the summit of Wilkerson Pass. The two summits are about 24 miles apart and close to the same elevation. The road between is not too steep for any long distance. It is all 2 lane with some 45 mph curves.

The westbound descent from Wilkerson Pass is about 6% for a short distance and then becomes more gradual and rolling. It is only 4 miles from the summit to Harstel in the valley floor. That is only a 647' drop in elevation in 4 miles. The road is 2 lane with 45 mph curves.

41 VAIL PASS elev. 10603'
(on I-70 east of Vail, CO)

The descent on the westbound side of Vail Pass is about 10 miles in length and begins at milepost 189 on I-70. One half mile west of the summit there are warning signs for westbound traffic--**"Speed limit 45 mph for vehicles over 30,000 lbs."** and **"Steep grade next 8 miles--trucks stay in lower gear."** The next mile is rolling hills. Then there is a sign--**"7% grade next 7 miles."**

The descent is **steady at 7%** and there are 3 advisory signs for the *first runaway truck ramp which is about milepost 185 or 4 miles down from the summit.* The escape ramp is upsloping on the right. *The second runaway truck ramp is about milepost 182, which is 3 1/4 miles after the first escape ramp, or about 7 1/4 miles down from the summit.* There are several advisory signs before reaching it and it is an upsloping ramp on the right. *Don't be fooled when the grade eases after the second escape ramp. It soon goes back to 7% and doesn't bottom out until 2 1/2 miles after the second escape ramp or about milepost 179.*

The eastbound descent from the summit of Vail Pass continues almost to the Frisco exit about 11 miles down the hill but the descent is not steady. There are short steep sections followed by short sections of lesser grade. The last half of the descent is 3-4% grade. *There are no escape ramps on the east side of the pass.*

42 WILKERSON PASS--see UTE PASS

COLORADO

43 WILLOW CREEK PASS elev. 9621'
(on Colorado Highway 125 south of Rand, CO)

Willow Creek Pass summit is about 10 miles south of Rand. The northbound descent from the summit is about **2 miles of 6% grade** with 30, 35, and 40 mph curves followed by about 2 1/2 miles of rolling hills. The southbound descent from the summit is about **7 1/2 miles of 5-6% grade** with many 35 and 40 mph curves followed by a mile or two of 3-4% grade.

44 WOLF CREEK PASS elev. 10850'
(on US 160 between South Fork and Pagosa Springs, CO)

Before beginning the climb on either side of Wolf Creek Pass there will be signs advising if chains or snow tires are required.

The eastbound descent from the summit of Wolf Creek Pass begins with a warning sign--**"6% grade next 8 miles."** Most of this is 3 lane road. Farther down the mountain the road alternates between 2 lane and 3 lane. **Vehicles over 55,000 lbs. 25 mph. speed limit.**

The descent begins with a 6% grade and 30 mph curves. About 2 miles down from the summit there is a short *tunnel* with a 30 mph curve. The grade continues as promised for about **8 miles at 6%** from the summit but there are about **2 more miles of 5%** before the grade eases enough to call it the end of the pass. There are 30 and 40 mph curves throughout the descent.

Going westbound from the summit of Wolf Creek Pass we find signs warning--**"7% grade-winding road next 9 miles"** and **"Trucks stay in lower gear"** and **"Vehicles over 55,000 lbs. must use right lane"** and **"Vehicles over 55,000 lbs. 25 mph."** Starting down the mountain westbound the speed limit is 25 mph. and it's 4 lane road. *There are two runaway truck ramps. They are 4 1/2 and 6 miles down from the summit of the pass, at mileposts 162 1/2 and 161.* After passing the second escape ramp **the 7% grade and 30 mph curves continue for another 2 miles** and then ease to a lesser grade for 2 miles before changing to rolling hills.

45 thru 49 see New Info on page 118.

COLORADO

RUNAWAY TRUCK RAMPS

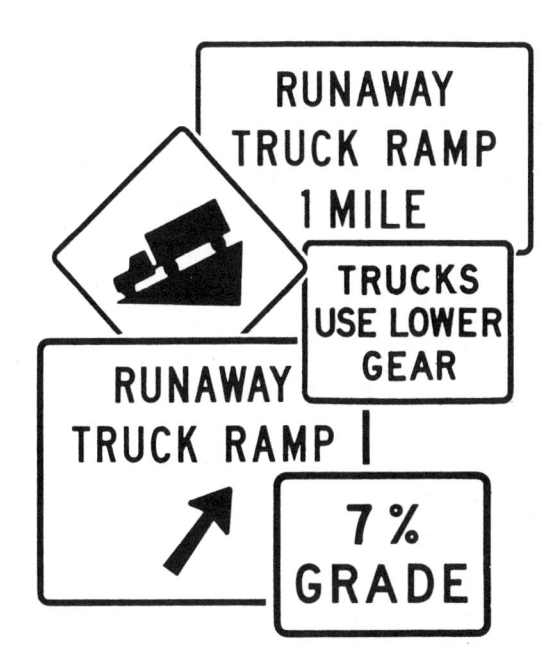

LOCATION MAP COLORADO TRUCK ESCAPE RAMPS

UPSLOPE STOPPING SYSTEM

- US 40 Rabbit Ears Pass
- I70 Vail Pass (Lower)
- I70 Vail Pass (Upper)
- I 70 Straight Creek (Lower)
- I 70 Straight Creek (Upper)
- US 160 Wolf Creek Pass (Lower)
- US 160 Wolf Creek Pass (Upper)
- US 50 Monarch Pass

* FLAT STOPPING SYSTEM

- I70 Mt. Vernon Canyon
- SH 141 Slick Rock Hill

* – These ramps are built on a grade that is the same or almost the same as the existing roadway. They utilize a gravel arrestor bed to slow down and gradually stop the truck.

FOR FURTHER INFORMATION CONTACT:

Colorado Motor Carriers Association
4060 Elati
Denver, CO 80216
433-3375

Colorado Department of Highways
Division of Highway Safety
4201 E. Arkansas Avenue
Denver, CO 80222
757-9381

Your nearest Colorado State Patrol Office.

Presented by:
Colorado Motor Carriers Association
Colorado Department of Highways
Division of Highway Safety
Colorado State Patrol

(Pages 45, 46, and 47 reproduced with permission)

(continued next page)

RUNAWAY TRUCK RAMPS

Colorado's Interstate highways and state roadways are lifelines for the people of this State. Coloradans use highways often in their daily lives - and they rely on the materials and goods moved by trucks using these roads. In Colorado, the trucking industry moves more goods through the State than any other transportation form.

With the increasing volume of trucks operating on Colorado roads, there has been an increase in the number of truck accidents and runaway trucks on mountain roads. There are many mountain highways in Colorado crossing the Continental Divide. Some of these roads have long descending grades ranging from 5 to 8 percent.

To prevent runaway truck accidents, escape ramps have been constructed at known problem locations (see map).

Reports of ramp usage and other runaway vehicle incidents provide the following information:

- 62% of the runaway trucks using the ramps are registered in states east of Colorado.
- 37% of the drivers utilizing the ramps have less than one year of mountain driving experience.
- 55% of the vehicles entering the ramps were in the 70 to 80 thousand pound gross vehicle weight range.

These statistics show a need for a greater awareness among truck drivers about the causes and prevention of runaway truck incidents and of the design and proper use of a escape ramp.

WHAT CAUSES RUNAWAYS?

Generally, brake fade (the loss of braking power).

Q. What is brake "Fade"?
A. It is a loss of braking power. It occurs when heat build-up causes the brake lining to glaze or deteriorate at high temperatures. This decreases the effectiveness of the brakes, and, in extreme cases, makes them nearly worthless.

Q. Are runaways becoming more prevalent?
A. Yes, for several reasons. These include:

- improper brake adjustment,
- reduction in natural vehicle retardation as vehicles are designed to reduce frictional resistance (i.e., radial tires, vehicle design, wind deflectors, etc.),
- changes in brake lining material, have lowered levels of braking power,
- over-reliance on the vehicle or trailer braking systems,
- disregard for the posted regulatory and warning signs - and the limitations of the vehicle and operator, and
- increases in traffic volumes.

Q. What can be done to prevent runaways?
A. These precautions will help:

- comply with posted regulatory and warning signs,
- operate a safe vehicle with a properly maintained braking system,
- when appropriate, descend the grade, **in a low gear,** utilizing the braking capabilities of the engine. (The common rule that says to go down a hill in the same gear you came up no longer applies, due to the increased horsepower in truck engines. The ability of your brakes to stop you on a downhill has not kept up with the engine's ability to take you up the hill).
- drive "ahead of yourself" to avoid the need for excessive use of the braking system, and
- operate the vehicle retarder or auxiliary retarder to provide full vehicle control - except for slowing down for occasional situations requiring use of the primary braking system.

TYPES OF RUNAWAY TRUCK RAMPS

There are four basic types of runaway truck escape ramps - sandpile, horizontal grade, descending grade, and ascending grade. Of these four types the Colorado Department of Highways has elected to use the ascending grade for eight locations and the descending grade type ramp for two locations. Research done by other states utilizing sandpile and windrow type arrestor beds indicated some

(pages 45, 46, and 47 reproduced with permission)

(continued next page)

COLORADO

evidence of damage; therefore, these designs were not employed. All ramps constructed in Colorado employ smooth arrestor beds of gravel 18 to 24 inches in depth.

ASCENDING GRADE

The ascending grade type ramps utilize both the arresting bed and the slowing (or up-hill) effect of gravity. These reduce the length of the ramp needed to stop the vehicle.

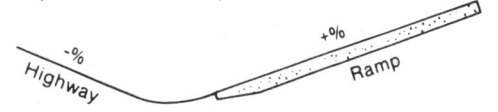

DESCENDING GRADE

For the descending grade type ramps the arrester bed is longer because gravity is not an element in reducing the speed of a vehicle. Any increase in rolling resistance to stop and slow the runaway vehicle is supplied by this longer gravel arresting bed.

USING A RUNAWAY RAMP

All ramps in Colorado are located on the right side of the roadway, are clearly identified with road sign advisory information and allow the driver a clear view of the entrance area.

When approaching the entrance, be certain the vehicle is centered on the ramp. Maintain a firm grip on the steering wheel during entry and keep the vehicle in the center of the ramp at all times.

DO NOT HESITATE IN USING THE RAMP. It has been designed to save your life. The ramp will stop your vehicle. The ramps have been used successfully by your fellow drivers.

The time to make your commitment is now-not under the stressful conditions during a runaway. The runaway truck escape ramp can save your life - and the lives of other people.

The escape ramps in Colorado have been designed to provide a direct access point where trucks can enter. There are special problems at the Mt. Vernon location (on I-70 just west of Denver). It is advisable to access this ramp from the entrace; however, if this is not possible (heavy volumes of traffic exist on this road) it has been used successfully by entering the ramp from the side. If this is necessary, it is recommended you try to go in as close to the entrance as possible to take the greatest advantage of the decelerating capabilities of the gravel arrestor bed.

(pages 45, 46, and 47 reproduced with permission)

IDAHO

▲ -- PASS OR STEEP GRADE LOCATIONS

IDAHO

1. 4TH OF JULY SUMMIT
2. ASHTON HILL
3. BANNER SUMMIT
4. BOISE HILL
   (see BANNER SUMMIT)
5. CHIEF JOSEPH PASS *
6. FISH CREEK PASS
7. GALENA SUMMIT
8. HORSESHOE BEND HILL
9. LEWISTON HILL
10. LOLO PASS *
11. LOOKOUT PASS *
12. LOST TRAIL PASS *
    (see CHIEF JOSEPH PASS)
13. McCALL HILL
14. MONIDA PASS *
15. MORES CREEK SUMMIT
    (see BANNER SUMMIT)
16. RAYNOLDS PASS *
17. TARGHEE PASS *
18. WHITE BIRD HILL
19. WILLOW CREEK DIVIDE
20. WINCHESTER HILL
21 thru 23 see New Info on page 118

* In both Idaho and Montana directories.

1   **4th OF JULY SUMMIT** elev. 3081'
(on I-90 east of Coeur D'Alene, ID)

The 4th of July Summit is about milepost 28 1/2 on I-90 east of Coeur D'Alene. Both sides of this hill are marked at **5 1/2% grade for 4 miles. The grade is steady** with 55 mph curves. There are chain up areas on both sides of the hill and warnings to beware of ice in the shady areas. There is also a truck pulloff area at the top of the hill.

2   **ASHTON HILL**
(on US 20 north of Ashton, ID)

The summit of Ashton Hill is about 6 miles north of Ashton on US 20. The north side of Ashton Hill has almost no descent but it does have a sign saying--**"Caution--moose on road at night next 40 miles."** The southbound descent from the top of Ashton Hill is 3 lane road with 55 mph speed limit and about **4 1/2 miles of steady 6% grade.**

49

IDAHO

3 BANNER SUMMIT elev. 7056'
(on Idaho Highway 21 west of Stanley, ID)
MORE'S CREEK SUMMIT elev. 6118'
(on Idaho Highway 21 west of Lowman, ID)
BOISE HILL
(on Idaho Highway 21 east of Boise, ID)

Idaho Highway 21 between Boise and Stanley **may be closed in winter.** Between Lowman and Idaho City there is a **65' length restriction.** Chains are advised between Lowman and Idaho City when it is snowy or icy.

Banner Summit is between Stanley and Lowman. Going east from the summit towards Stanley there are some short 3-4% hills to descend but mostly it's rolling hills with 55 mph speed limit.

Going west from the summit there is about 3/4 mile of 3-4% grade and then a sign saying--"**6% grade next 3 miles."** The speed limit is 55 mph and the grade seems to continue at **6% for about 4 miles and then another mile of 5%** with 40 mph curves. The grade then varies from 3% to 5% for several miles. The road then rolls up and down for about 25 miles with long gentle hills or short steep hills. This continues to Lowman.

Continuing west out of Lowman, highway 21 becomes narrow and winding for many miles. It also begins a steep climb with **4-6% grades for almost 10 miles** to a summit with no name. The curves are continuous at about 20 to 25 mph, some of them hairpins. The westbound descent from this summit with no name is also a winding road. The downhill grade starts at about 5% but a mile or so later begins to lessen to about 4%, then 3%, then 2% until 5 miles down the hill you bottom out and start uphill toward the More's Creek Summit.

The next 2 1/2 miles are rolling hills in the 4-5% range. Then the grade goes to a **steady 5-6% uphill for about 3 miles to More's Creek Summit.**

The trip down the west side of More's Creek Summit is more curves and hairpin turns at 20 to 25 mph and steady **5-6% grade for about 5 miles** followed by 3 miles of 3-4% before the road opens up to about 40 mph speed limit. A few miles later you are in Idaho City.

Might as well go on to Boise. A few miles east of Boise on highway 21 is a hill with **4 miles of 6%** on the west side of the summit and about **2 miles of 6%** on the east side. This hill is just east of Barber Dam.

4 BOISE HILL--see BANNER SUMMIT

5 CHIEF JOSEPH PASS elev. 7264'
(on Montana Highway 43 west of Wisdom, MT)
LOST TRAIL PASS elev. 7014'
(on US 93 west of Butte, MT on the Montana-Idaho state line)

The eastbound descent from the summit of Chief Joseph Pass is about 2 1/2 miles of 4-5% grade and then a couple more miles at 2-3%. The road then remains almost level for many miles. It is a good 2 lane road.

Traveling west on State 43 over Chief Joseph Pass the descent from the summit is only about 1 mile of 5-6% grade. At the end of this mile you come to the junction of State 43 and US 93. This junction is the summit of Lost Trail Pass, so whether you go north or south there is more descent.

At the time of this writing (Sept. 1993) there is road construction on both sides of Lost Trail Pass. It appears the road is being widened to 3 lane. Some sections are completed. There is a sign at the summit for southbound trucks warning of a 65' length limit. This may or may not be due to construction and local inquiry should be made.

From the summit southbound there are numerous sharp curves and about **6% grade for about 3 1/2 miles.** The road then becomes more narrow and there is a **5% grade warning sign.** It remains a very curvy road. About 2 miles later the grade eases somewhat and remains in the 3-4% range for about 8 more miles. There is some rolling but it is mostly downhill at least as far as Gibbonsville.

The northbound descent from the summit of Lost Trail Pass has 25 and 30 mph curves and is a pretty **steady 5-6% descent for about 7 miles** and then there are about 2 more miles of lesser grade.

6 FISH CREEK PASS
(on US 30 between Lund and Lava Hot Springs, ID)

The east side of Fish Creek Pass is a 4 lane road with a descent of about **5-6% for 2 miles.**

The westbound descent from the summit begins as 4 lane and then 3 lane and finally 2 lane about the time Lava Hot Springs is reached. It is a **5-6% downgrade for almost 5 miles. There are two runaway truck ramps.** The first is about 1 1/2 miles down from the summit. It exits to the right and is at the same grade as the road--where the shoulder would normally be. The second runaway truck ramp is 1 1/2 miles after the first or 3 miles down from the summit. It also exits to the right (in the middle of a curve) and is where the shoulder would normally be. About 4 1/2 miles down from the summit is the town of Lava Hot Springs where the grade begins to ease.

IDAHO

7 GALENA SUMMIT elev. 8701'
(on Idaho Highway 75 north of Ketchum, ID)

The top of Galena Summit is at milepost 158 on state highway 75 which is a good, smooth 2 lane road. Starting south from the summit there is a sign warning--**"6% grade next 8 miles."** It certainly is **6% for about 5 miles** but it appears as though the grade eases to 3-4% about 5 miles down from the summit and 6 1/2 miles down from the summit it seems to be about 1-2% and the speed limit is back to 55 mph. Starting at the very top there are sharp curves all the way down thru that 6 1/2 miles of descent. Most are about 30 mph curves and they are almost continuous.

The northbound descent begins with a warning sign--**"6% grade next 5 miles."** There are 30, 35, and 40 mph curves all the way down this side as well. The grade is pretty **steady at 6%** for most of the promised 5 miles.

8 HORSESHOE BEND HILL elev. 4242'
(on Idaho Highway 55 north of Boise and south of Horseshoe Bend, ID)

The summit of Horseshoe Bend Hill is at milepost 57 on state highway 55. This is about 6 miles south of the town of Horseshoe Bend. Going south from the summit toward Boise there are about **3 miles of 5-6% downhill**, a 2 mile stretch where the grade eases, and then **2 more miles of 6%**.

The northbound descent from the summit is **7% for 5 miles and then 3/4 mile of 6%** *with 4 runaway truck ramps spaced about a mile apart* as you descend towards Horseshoe Bend. The first three escape ramps are upsloping. The last slopes down at about the same grade as the road. *Use it if you have any doubts about your brakes because at the bottom of this hill the 4 lane turns to 2 lane as you enter the edge of town. **The speed limit drops to 35 mph and shortly after that there is a school zone.*** The **truck speed limit is 35 mph all the way down** from the summit. ***Use caution on this hill.***

9 LEWISTON HILL
(on US 95 just north of Lewiston, ID)

The top of Lewiston Hill is at milepost 318 1/2 on US 95 north of Lewiston. There is very little descent on the north side of this hill.

There is a weigh station and steep grade information for southbounders at the top of the hill. The **speed limit for trucks is 35 mph** on the south side of the hill. The downhill grade is a **steady 7% for 6 miles**. There are *three runaway truck ramps. They are 3, 4 3/4, and 5 1/4 miles down from the summit.* The grade continues all the way down into Lewiston with 45 mph curves the last 4 miles.

IDAHO

10 LOLO PASS elev. 5235'
(on US 12 west of Missoula, MT at the Montana-Idaho state line)

US 12 highway over Lolo Pass is a pretty good 2 lane road. There is a truck turnout area at the summit for brake checks and chain up areas at the bottom of the grades. As with many mountain passes it is a winding road with many 35 and 40 mph curves.

At the summit there is a truck warning sign for eastbounders--**"5% grade next 4 miles."** The first couple of miles are 5% and then the grade eases to 3-4% for just a short while and then goes back to 5% for another mile or so. This whole descent is winding and remains so after the chain up area is passed but the grade pretty much flattens out at this point.

Going west from the summit a truck warning sign says--**"6% grade next 5 miles--trucks 35 mph."** It is a **steady descent at 6%** with many 35 and 40 mph curves. After 5 miles of 6% there are about 3 miles of lesser grade before the road begins to roll and then level out.

About a mile down from the summit is a sign--**"Winding road next 77 miles."** Yes, that is seventy-seven.

11 LOOKOUT PASS elev. 4725'
(on I-90 at the Montana-Idaho state line)

The Idaho side of Lookout Pass has about **5 miles of 5-6% descent** and then several more miles of lesser grade. There are *two runaway truck ramps.* There is a sign at the summit for westbounders--**"Truckers--steep grade next 5 miles--6% maximum--check brakes."** The first couple of miles down are 6%. There is a sign 2 1/4 miles down saying--**"5% grade next 3 miles."**

The *first escape ramp is 3 1/2 miles down from the summit.* It goes downhill and curves to the right. *The second escape ramp is 1 mile after the first.* It is on the right side at the same grade as the road-- where the right shoulder would normally be. About 6 miles down the hill the grade eases. The downhill continues for many miles but not nearly so steep.

The eastbound descent is about **6% for 2 miles then eases to 5% for about 1 mile** and then eases even more. The chain removal area is about 4 1/2 miles down from the summit. The descent from this point is gradual for another 10 miles or so.

12 LOST TRAIL PASS--see CHIEF JOSEPH PASS

13 McCALL HILL
(on Idaho Highway 55 between McCall and Meadows, ID)

Immediately after leaving McCall going north on highway 55 there is a chain up area. The climb to the top of the hill is only about **2 miles at 3-5% grade.**

The descent on the north side starts at about 5% for 1/2 mile, then 3% for 1/2 mile, and back to 5% for 1/2 mile. At this point there is a warning sign--**"7% grade next 3 miles--use lower gear."** About 3/4 mile later 25 mph curves begin and the grade goes to 7%. The curves are sharp and continuous as is the grade for about 2 1/2 miles. The grade eases and then bottoms out about 1/2 mile later. This road is all 2 lane.

IDAHO

14 MONIDA PASS elev. 6870'
(on I-15 at Idaho-Montana state line)

Monida is one of those passes you hardly know you've been over. It is a good 2 lane road with 65 mph speed limit. There is about 1 mile of 3% grade on each side of the summit and then a very gradual rolling descent that goes on for miles on both sides of the pass.

15 MORE'S CREEK SUMMIT--see BANNER SUMMIT

16 RAYNOLDS PASS elev. 6836'
(at the Montana-Idaho state line on Highway 87)

This highway has the same number (87) in both Montana and Idaho.

Raynolds Pass summit is at the border of Montana and Idaho which is also the Continental Divide. The signs for the border and the Continental Divide are about the only clues to the whereabouts of the summit. There is really no discernable climb or descent--only rolling hills in both directions.

17 TARGHEE PASS elev. 7072'
(on US 20 west of Yellowstone National Park on the Idaho-Montana state line)

Targhee Pass is on the Montana-Idaho state line just west of Yellowstone National Park. The east side of the pass is about 1 1/2 miles of 4-6% grade. The west side is about 2 1/2 miles of 4-6% grade. It is all 2 lane road with 55 mph speed limit. It seems like a very mild mannered pass but a Montana state trooper indicated there are many accidents on this pass in the winter months.

18 WHITE BIRD HILL elev. 4245'
(on US 95 south of Grangeville, ID)

The summit of White Bird Hill is about 8 miles south of Grangeville. This is a long, steep hill going south. The northbound descent is only about **2 1/2 miles of 6-7% grade** with 55 mph speed limit.

The southbound descent is **8 miles of 7% grade with 3 runaway truck ramps. The speed limit for trucks is 35 mph.** The road alternates from 2 lane to 3 lane. Most of the south side of the hill is 3 lane. *There is a truck turnout for brake checks about 1/2 mile below the summit on the south side. There are numerous signs about speed limit for trucks, grade and length warnings, and runaway truck ramp warnings.*

The runaway truck ramps are 1 1/2, 3, and 6 1/2 miles down from the summit. All are upsloping ramps. **The grade does last for the promised 8 miles** with a 2 lane bridge at the bottom of the hill. ***This is a dangerous hill for large and heavy vehicles. Use caution.***

SCRATCH HERE
IF YOU DON'T SMELL BURNING BRAKES YOU MUST OWN A

MOUNTAIN TAMER
VARIABLE ENGINE BRAKING
GAS AND DIESEL
Also High Performance Torque Converters

DECEL-O-MATIC CORP
SEE AD ON PAGE 3

IDAHO

19 WILLOW CREEK DIVIDE elev. 7160'
(on US 93 south of Challis, ID)

The summit of Willow Creek Divide is about 23 miles south of Challis. US 93 is a two lane road that could stand to be a little wider and has no paved shoulder.

The northbound descent from the summit begins with a couple of miles of 3-4% grade and then a long gradual rolling descent for many miles. There is a rock canyon about 10 miles north of the summit where the grade goes to 4-5% for about a mile or so. The road surface in this canyon probably doesn't get much sun to melt ice and snow so it may be slick when the rest of the road is dry. It is only about 1 1/2 miles thru the canyon.

The southbound descent from the summit starts with about 1 1/2 miles of 4-5% grade. At this point the grade eases for about 1/2 mile and then goes downhill at 3-4% for about 3 more miles.

20 WINCHESTER HILL
(on US 95 north of Winchester, ID)

This hill is a northbound descent starting at about milepost 279 on US 95 north of Winchester. Winchester is just south of Lewiston, Idaho. The sign at the top says--**"6% grade next 4 miles." This 4 miles of 6% is followed by 2 miles of 5% and then 2 miles of 4%.** It is 2 lane road.

21 thru 23 see New Info on page 118.

WESTERN MONTANA

▲ — PASS OR STEEP GRADE LOCATIONS

MONTANA

1. BEAR TOOTH PASS *
2. CHIEF JOSEPH PASS **
3. COLTER PASS *
   (see BEAR TOOTH PASS)
4. DEER LODGE PASS
5. ELK PARK PASS
6. FLESHER PASS
7. FLINT CREEK HILL
8. HOMESTAKE PASS
9. LOGAN PASS
10. LOLO PASS **
11. LOOKOUT PASS **
12. LOST TRAIL PASS **
    (see CHIEF JOSEPH PASS)
13. MacDONALD PASS
14. MARIAS PASS
15. MONIDA PASS **
16. PIPESTONE PASS
17. RAYNOLDS PASS **
18. ROGERS PASS
19. TARGHEE PASS **
20. VIRGINIA CITY--ENNIS HILL

* In both Montana and Wyoming directories.
** In both Idaho and Montana directories.

1   **BEAR TOOTH PASS** elev. 10947' and **COLTER PASS** elev. 8000'
(on US 212 west of Red Lodge, Mt)

Bear Tooth Pass is aptly named. It is a bear of a pass. The Montana-Wyoming state line is near the summit. The Montana side of the pass is the most difficult with a very narrow, rough, winding, and steep descent. **The pass is usually closed to winter travel** and in any season the weather can change rapidly. Bear Tooth Pass has an east summit and a west summit. The descent from the west summit to the bottom on the Montana side (in other words-eastbound) is **22 miles of 6-8% grade.** The road is narrow and there are few places one can pull over alongside the road if need be. There are numerous 15, 20, 25 mph hairpin turns, many of these unmarked.

Descending eastbound from the west summit of Bear Tooth the first 1 1/2 miles are about 8% downhill grade followed by 1 1/2 miles of 5-7% grade uphill to the east summit.

The **first 4 miles downhill from the east summit are about 8%** with 20 mph hairpins and other curves. At the end of the 4 miles there is a sign stating--**"Winding road next 15 miles."** The worst of it only lasts about **10 miles.** This is **steady 5-6% grade,** almost continuous 15 to 25 mph curves, and narrow road with very little shoulder. After this 10 mile section the road opens up a little with speed limits increased to about 50 mph but the **grade is still in the 5-6% range for another 3-4 miles.** *Brakes may be hot by this time--use caution about increasing speed.* The grade will begin to ease after the 3-4 miles of 50 mph speed limits and the descent will be completed about 7 miles west of Red Lodge, Montana.

The westbound descent from the west summit of Bear Tooth is **about 6-7% grade** but it is not as steady as the Montana side. There are some places where the grade eases or nearly flattens for short stretches--maybe as little as 1/4 mile--and then goes back down. There are many 15, 20, 25 mph hairpin turns and curves--some unmarked--and the road does not improve until about 13 miles down from the summit where it gets wider and smoother. About 18 1/2 miles down from the summit is a sharp curve with a bridge in the middle of it. If you are from a cold climate you already know that bridges can be icy when the rest of the road is not. This bridge could be a problem in bad weather.

(continued)

MONTANA

(Bear Tooth Pass continued)

Some of the steeper sections of this descent are farther down the mountain. The total trip down is about **21 miles** and the last few miles have some grade in the **7-8% range.**

If you continue westbound you will go over Colter Pass but after Bear Tooth you probably won't even notice it. Colter Pass summit is about 1 1/2 miles east of Cooke City and about 5 miles east of Yellowstone Park's entrance. The road is rolling throughout this area and there are no long climbs or descents on either side of Colter Pass.

2   **CHIEF JOSEPH PASS** elev. 7264'
(on Montana Highway 43 west of Wisdom, MT)
LOST TRAIL PASS elev. 7014'
(on US 93 west of Butte, MT on the Montana-Idaho state line)

The eastbound descent from the summit of Chief Joseph Pass is about 2 1/2 miles of 4-5% grade and then a couple more miles at 2-3%. The road then remains almost level for many miles. It is a good 2 lane road.

Traveling west on State 43 over Chief Joseph Pass the descent from the summit is only about 1 mile of 5-6% grade. At the end of this mile you come to the junction of State 43 and US 93. This junction is the summit of Lost Trail Pass, so whether you go north or south there is more descent.

At the time of this writing (Sept. 1993) there is road construction on both sides of Lost Trail Pass. It appears the road is being widened to 3 lane. Some sections are completed. There is a sign at the summit for southbound trucks warning of a 65' length limit. This may or may not be due to construction and local inquiry should be made.

From the summit southbound there are numerous sharp curves and about **6% grade for about 3 1/2 miles.** The road then becomes more narrow and there is a **5% grade warning sign**. It remains a very curvy road. About 2 miles later the grade eases somewhat and remains in the 3-4% range for about 8 more miles. There is some rolling but it is mostly downhill at least as far as Gibbonsville.

The northbound descent from the summit of Lost Trail Pass has 25 and 30 mph curves and is a pretty **steady 5-6% descent for about 7 miles** and then there is about 2 more miles of lesser grade.

3   **COLTER PASS**--see BEAR TOOTH PASS

4   **DEER LODGE PASS** elev. 5902'
(on I-15 south of I-90 near Butte, MT)

The summit of Deer Lodge Pass is where I-15 crosses the Continental Divide about 9 miles south of the junction of I-15 and I-90. It is not easy to distinguish the top of this pass because it looks like all the other hills between I-90 and Melrose, which is 28 miles south of I-90. These hills are often in the 5-6% range but they usually aren't over a mile or so in length.

The road is 4 lane with regular interstate speed limits and mostly long sweeping curves. The exception to this is exit 99 at Moose Creek. The curves get much sharper at this exit. At the bottom of the hill and in the middle of these sharper curves are bridges for each side of I-15. These bridges could be a problem in snowy or icy conditions. A Montana state trooper indicated there are frequent truck accidents along this stretch of road.

5 ELK PARK PASS
(on I-15 at the north edge of Butte, MT)

Elk Park Pass is one sided with a **3 mile 6% grade** descending into Butte from the north on I-15. The descent begins at milepost 133 and continues to milepost 130 where you can go west on I-15/90 or east on I-90. If you go east on I-90 the descent continues another 1/2 mile where the road becomes one lane and goes under a bridge and makes a sharp right turn and becomes the ramp onto I-90 eastbound.

There is no descent on the north side of Elk Park Pass.

6 FLESHER PASS elev. 6130'
(on Montana Highway 279 north of Helena, MT)

The descent on the north side of Flesher Pass starts with about a **mile of 6-7% grade then eases to 5-6% for about 2 1/2 miles** where it levels out. The grade then goes back down and then levels out. This stairstepping pattern is repeated for several miles until the junction with state highway 200 is reached 8 miles down from the summit. Most of the curves on this side are about 30 mph.

The southbound descent from the summit of Flesher Pass is about **3 1/2 miles of mostly 6%** with one section of steeper grade that is only about 1/4 mile long. There are 20, 30, and 35 mph curves. After the 3 1/2 miles of descent the road begins rolling up and down and continues almost to Canyon Creek, 12 miles to the south.

7 FLINT CREEK HILL
(on Montana Highway 1 just north of Georgetown Lake, MT)

Georgetown Lake is west of Anaconda, Montana on State highway 1. Flint Creek Hill begins its descent near the dam on the north end of the lake. The 2 lane road enters a canyon and descends at **6-7% for almost 3 miles**. There are 30 mph curves.

MONTANA

8   HOMESTAKE PASS elev. 6375'
(on I-90 east of Butte, MT)

Homestake Pass has two summits about 2 miles apart and between them is a valley with a rest area in it. *Trucks traveling east are asked to stop in this rest area for grade information.* The rest area is at milepost 235. The sign in the rest area reads as follows: **"Danger area--5 miles of 6% downgrade with curves--fatal truck accidents have occurred between mileposts 235 and 241. You are advised to check your vehicle's braking system and make safety checks. You are advised to proceed at low speed between rest area and bottom of the hill.** *Runaway truck ramp between milepost 238 and 239."* A Montana state trooper indicated there has been a significant decrease in the number of *truck accidents since the posting of the warning sign and the reduction in the truck speed limit.*

By the time you begin the downhill grade on the east side the truck speed limit is down to **25 mph for vehicles over 12,000 lbs.** There are 50 mph curves and the *runaway truck ramp* is where they promised it would be--*at milepost 238 1/2*.

There is a series of curves toward the end of the grade and the truck speed limit goes to 35 and then 45 and then up to normal speed limits. The grade ends almost 6 miles down from where it started.

The westbound descent into Butte is about **3 miles of steady 6% grade.** There are no special truck speed limits on this side of the hill. On both sides of the hill there are chain up and chain removal areas big enough to accommodate 2-3 trucks.

9   LOGAN PASS elev. 6646'--also known as GOING TO THE SUN ROAD
(in Glacier National Park, MT)

Vehicles over 24' in length are prohibited on the pass in 1993 and vehicles over 20' in length will be prohibited in 1994. This is truly a spectacular drive, especially on the west side of the summit. There are tour busses available if your vehicle is over-length. The road was built in the 1920's and 30's and is very narrow and winding in places.

The eastbound descent from the summit of Logan Pass is about **6 miles of 5-6% grade** followed by several more miles of lesser grade and rolling hills. The westbound descent is longer with about **9 miles of 5-6% grade** and then 2 or 3 miles of more gradual descent. There are many stretches of narrow road, especially noticeable in the sharp curves.

10   LOLO PASS elev. 5235'
(on US 12 west of Missoula, MT at the Montana-Idaho state line)

US 12 highway over Lolo Pass is a pretty good 2 lane road. There is a truck turnout area at the summit for brake checks and chain up areas at the bottom of the grades. As with many mountain passes it is a winding road with many 35 and 40 mph curves.

At the summit there is a truck warning sign for eastbounders--**"5% grade next 4 miles."** The first couple of miles are 5% and then the grade eases to 3-4% for just a short while and then goes back to 5% for another mile or so. This whole descent is winding and remains so after the chain up area is passed but the grade pretty much flattens out at this point.

Going west from the summit a truck warning sign says--**"6% grade next 5 miles--trucks 35 mph."** It is a **steady descent at 6%** with many 35 and 40 mph curves. After 5 miles of 6% there are about 3 miles of lesser grade before the road begins to roll and then level out. About a mile down from the summit is a sign--**"Winding road next 77 miles."** Yes, that is seventy-seven.

MONTANA

11 LOOKOUT PASS elev. 4725'
(on I-90 at the Montana-Idaho state line)

The Idaho side of Lookout Pass has about **5 miles of 5-6% descent** and then several more miles of lesser grade. There are **two runaway truck ramps.** There is a sign at the summit for westbounders--**"Truckers--steep grade next 5 miles--6% maximum--check brakes."** The first couple of miles down are 6%. There is a sign 2 1/4 miles down saying--**"5% grade next 3 miles."**

The **first escape ramp is 3 1/2 miles down from the summit.** It goes downhill and curves to the right. The **second escape ramp is 1 mile after the first.** It is on the right side at the same grade as the road-- where the right shoulder would normally be. About 6 miles down the hill the grade eases. The downhill continues for many miles but not nearly so steep.

The eastbound descent is about **6% for 2 miles then eases to 5% for about 1 mile** and then eases even more. The chain removal area is about 4 1/2 miles down from the summit. The descent from this point is gradual for another 10 miles or so.

12 LOST TRAIL PASS--see CHIEF JOSEPH PASS

13 MAC DONALD PASS   elev. 6320'
(on US 12 west of Helena, MT)

The summit of MacDonald Pass is about 13 miles west of Helena. US 12 is a 4 lane road from Helena to the bottom of the pass on the west side. There are chain up and chain removal areas on both sides of the pass.

The westbound descent from the summit begins with about **3/4 mile of 8%** downgrade. There are **no truck warnings going west.** After the first 3/4 mile the grade eases to **6-7% for about 2 miles, then goes to about 5% the last 1/2 mile** to the chain removal area. The road then becomes 2 lane and flattens out. From the summit to the chain removal area is about 4 1/2 miles.

The descent on the east side is steeper and longer. *There are no escape ramps*. The eastbound descent begins with a truck warning sign--**"Steep grade 6 miles--advise 25 mph maximum"** and **"8% next 6 miles."** And indeed it is **very steep and steady for 6 miles**. The chain removal area is 6.1 miles down from the summit.

14 MARIAS PASS elev. 5280'
(on US 2 at the south edge of Glacier National Park, MT)

The east side of Marias Pass is just rolling hills. It doesn't seem like a pass at all. The hills farther east between East Glacier and Browning are much steeper than the hills on the east side of this pass. The west side of the pass has about 3-4 miles of descent that varies from 3 to 6% followed by miles of lesser grade. It is a good 2 lane road with no truck warning signs in either direction.

SCRATCH HERE

IF YOU *DON'T* SMELL BURNING BRAKES YOU MUST OWN A

MOUNTAIN TAMER
VARIABLE ENGINE BRAKING
GAS AND DIESEL
Also High Performance Torque Converters

DECEL-O-MATIC CORP
SEE AD ON PAGE 3

MONTANA

15 MONIDA PASS elev. 6870'
(on I-15 at Idaho-Montana state line)

Monida is one of those passes you hardly know you've been over. It is a good 2 lane road with 65 mph speed limit. There is about 1 mile of 3% grade on each side of the summit and then a very gradual rolling descent that goes on for miles on both sides of the pass.

16 PIPESTONE PASS elev. 6453'
(on Montana Highway 2 south of Butte, MT)

Montana State Highway 2 is a winding two lane road south of Butte. From the summit of Pipestone westbound there is only about **2 or 3 miles of 5-6% descent** with curves from 15 to 35 mph.

Going east from the summit there is a **5-6% descent for almost 8 miles.** Much of this is fairly steady grade but there are a couple of sections of rolling hills. The curves are not as sharp as on the west side.

17 RAYNOLDS PASS elev. 6836'
(at the Montana-Idaho state line on Highway 87)

This highway has the same number (87) in both Montana and Idaho.

Raynolds Pass summit is at the border of Montana and Idaho which is also the Continental Divide. The signs for the border and the Continental Divide are about the only clues to the whereabouts of the summit. There is really no discernable climb or descent--only rolling hills in both directions.

18 ROGERS PASS elev. 5610'
(on Montana Highway 200 north of Helena, MT)

Traveling west on State 200 there are no truck warning signs at the summit of Rogers Pass. There is only about 1 mile of about 6% descent and then 5% and less for about 2 miles to the chain up area. The road continues to roll up and down west of there.

The eastbound descent begins with a sign saying--"6%"--no other details. It is a **steady 6% descent for about 3 miles** with 25 mph curves near the top. The grade eases to about 5% and then begins to roll up and down. This continues for many miles with some 5-7% hills included but they are usually short in length.

19 TARGHEE PASS elev. 7072'
(on US 20 west of Yellowstone National Park on Idaho-Montana state line)

Targhee Pass is on the Montana-Idaho state line just west of Yellowstone National Park. The east side of the pass is about 1 1/2 miles of 4-6% grade. The west side is about 2 1/2 miles of 4-6% grade. It is all 2 lane road with 55 mph speed limit. It seems like a very mild mannered pass but a Montana state trooper indicated there are many accidents on this pass in the winter months.

20 ENNIS--VIRGINIA CITY HILL
(on Montana Highway 287 between Ennis and; Virginia City, MT)

This hill is not called a pass or even acknowledged on most maps but it should be driven with as much caution as many mountain passes.

The descent from the summit heading east begins with about **1 mile of 6-7%** downhill grade. Then the grade eases for a mile and then back down at a fairly **steady 5-7% for about 4 miles**. Again the grade eases for about 1 mile before the last steep 1/2 mile. It is 10 miles from the summit to Ennis.

Heading west from the summit a sign says--**"7% grade next 3 miles--trucks use lower gear."** And indeed it is a steep grade. After 1 mile of descent there is a sign--*"Runaway truck ramp 1/2 mile."* The escape ramp is on the right shoulder at about the same grade as the road. It is almost 1/2 mile long. **The grade remains in the 7% range** and the speed limit drops from 45 mph to 35 and then to 25 as you approach Virginia City. The grade eases some as you come into town but remains **5-6% right thru town.** It flattens out more after leaving the west side of town.

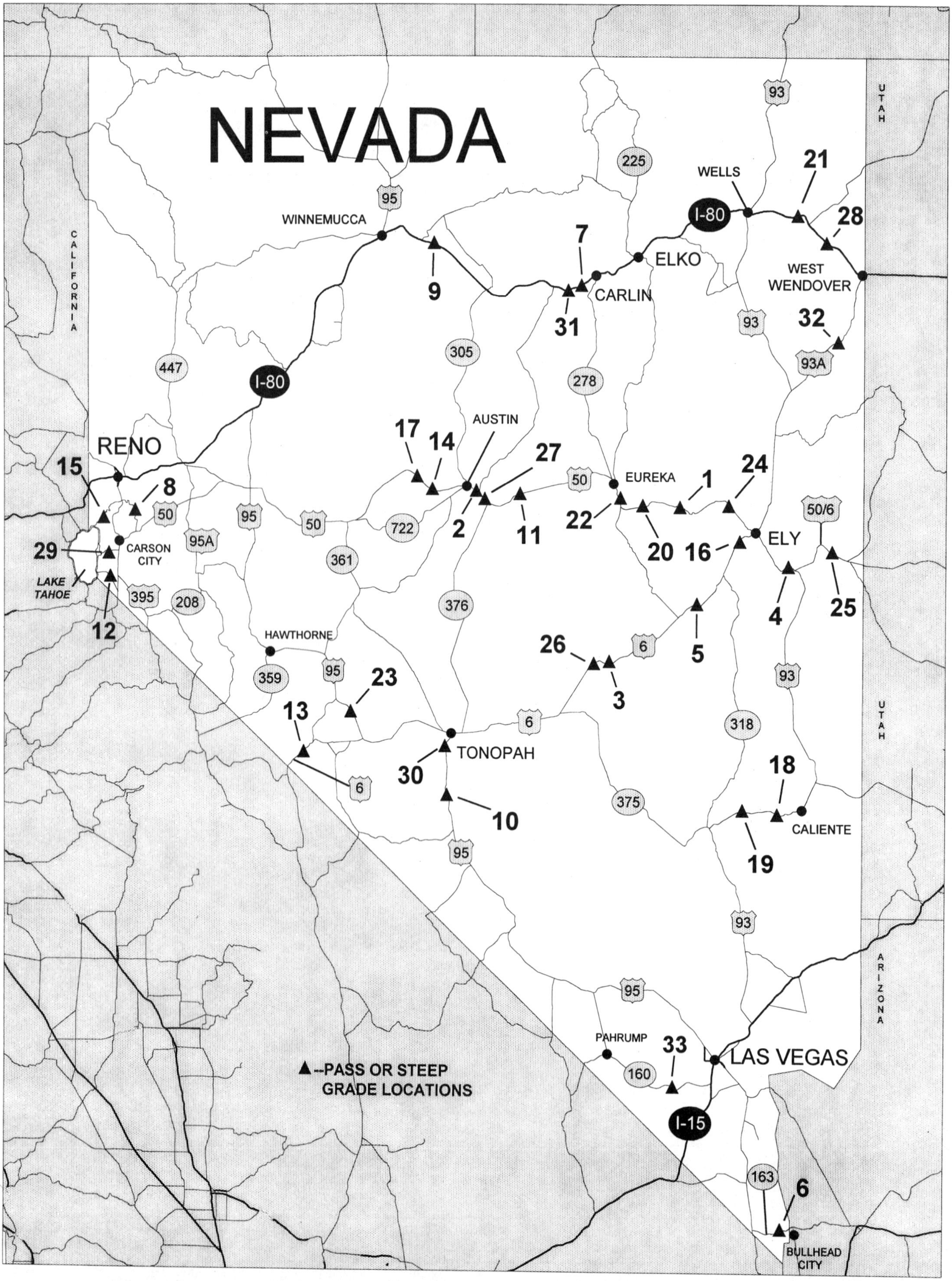

MapInfo® is the registered trademark of MapInfo Corporation, Troy, New York

NEVADA

1. ANTELOPE SUMMIT
2. AUSTIN SUMMIT
   (see SCOTT SUMMIT)
3. BLACKROCK SUMMIT
   (see SANDY SUMMIT)
4. CONNORS PASS
5. CURRANT SUMMIT
6. DAVIS DAM HILL
7. EMIGRANT SUMMIT
8. GEIGER GRADE
9. GOLCONDA SUMMIT
10. GOLDFIELD SUMMIT
11. HICKISON SUMMIT
12. KINGSBERRY GRADE
13. MONTGOMERY PASS
14. MT. AIRY SUMMIT
15. MT. ROSE SUMMIT
16. MURRAY SUMMIT
17. NEW PASS SUMMIT
    (see MT. AIRY SUMMIT)
18. OAK SPRINGS SUMMIT
19. PAHROC SUMMIT
20. PANCAKE SUMMIT
21. PEQUOP SUMMIT
22. PINTO SUMMIT
23. REDLICH SUMMIT
24. ROBINSON SUMMIT
25. SACRAMENTO PASS
26. SANDY SUMMIT
27. SCOTT SUMMIT
28. SILVER ZONE PASS
    (see PEQUOP SUMMIT)
29. SPOONER SUMMIT
30. TONOPAH SUMMIT
31. TWIN SUMMIT
    (see EMIGRANT SUMMIT)
32. WHITE HORSE PASS
33. See New Info on page 118

1 ANTELOPE SUMMIT elev. 7433'
(on US 50 between Eureka and Ely, NV)

The eastbound descent from Antelope Summit starts with about 1/4 mile of 5% grade and then eases to 1-3% for almost 10 miles. There is some winding road with 45 mph curves.

The westbound descent starts with 35 mph curves and 4-6% grade for about 2 miles. The grade then eases and stairsteps down at about 3% for another 7 miles. There is one very short section of 6%--just about 1/4 mile long near the top of the 7 mile stretch.

2 AUSTIN SUMMIT--see SCOTT SUMMIT

3 BLACK ROCK SUMMIT--see SANDY SUMMIT

Instant Power You can FEEL! Improves Acceleration, Hill Climbing & Passing!

GIBSON PERFORMANCE EXHAUST SYSTEMS

Complete Exhaust Systems...from Headers to Stainless Steel tip
TRUCKS and MOTORHOMES! • Lowest Price/Highest Quality
Aluminized & Stainless Bolt-on Kits • 50 State Legal • Lifetime Warranty

GIBSON PERFORMANCE EXHAUST SYSTEMS

714/528-3044 • FREE CATALOG • 800/528-3044

4 CONNORS PASS elev. 7723'
(on US 93/50/6 east of Ely, NV)

Conners Pass summit is about 21 miles east of Ely. The westbound descent from the summit begins with about 1 1/2 miles of 6% grade and 45 mph curves, and then eases to 2-4% for 2 more miles.

The eastbound descent begins with a truck warning sign--**"Trucks use lower gear."** The grade is about **6% for 4 1/2 miles** to the junction where US 93 splits from US 50/6. There are 45 mph curves down to the junction where the road opens up. The grade eases to about 3-4% at the junction.

If you follow US 93 the grade is 3-4% for about 1 1/2 miles. If you follow US 50/6 the descent goes to 4-5% after the junction for about 2 miles and then 3-4% for another 1 1/2 miles.

5 CURRANT SUMMIT elev. 6999'
(on US 6 east of Currant, NV)

Currant Summit is about 12 1/2 miles east of Currant, Nevada. The descent westbound from the summit starts with 1 mile of 6% grade. The rest of the distance to Currant is only 1-3% grade with some 30 and 45 mph curves. The descent eastbound from the summit starts with about 1 1/2 miles of 6% grade and then 2-4% for the next 10 miles. There are 45 mph curves.

6 DAVIS DAM HILL
(on Nevada state highway 163 east of the junction with US 95)

About 12 miles east of the junction of state highway 163 and US 95 the descent to Davis Dam begins. It is about **7 1/2 miles of 6% grade** with 50 mph curves. The road is 4 lane for the first 5 miles and then goes to 2 lane near the turnoff to Laughlin, Nevada. The grade continues almost to the dam at the Arizona state line.

7 EMIGRANT SUMMIT elev. 6114' and TWIN SUMMITS elev. 5672'
(on I-80 west of Carlin, NV)

Emigrant Summit is about 9 miles west of Carlin at milepost 271. The descent westbound starts with about **3 miles of grade that varies from 3 to 5%, mostly 4-5%**. The next 10 miles are up and down with two more unmarked summits. According to the map these must be Twin Summits. The up and down grades vary from 2 to 5%. The 4-5% sections are 1 1/2 miles or less in length with stretches of lesser grade or uphill road breaking up the descent.

The eastbound descent from Emigrant Summit is in stages with grades that vary from 2 to 6%. The 6% section is preceded by a sign saying--**"Trucks use lower gear"** and lasts about 1 1/2 miles and then eases to about 3-4% for another mile. The rest of the grade is in the 2-4% range with rolling hills near the bottom.

8 GEIGER GRADE elev. 6799'
(on Nevada Highway 341 between Reno and Virginia City, NV)

The summit of Geiger Grade is about 9 miles south of the junction of 341 and US 395.

The northbound descent begins with about **1 1/2 miles of 6% grade**. The grade eases for about 1/2 mile and then begins a **steady 5-6% descent for about 6 miles**. The 25 and 30 mph curves are almost continuous. This is a hazardous road in bad weather with steep drop offs along the side.

The southbound descent to Virginia City is a rolling grade about **3 1/2 miles long. It is mostly 5-6% grade** with several short stretches of lesser grade. It is uphill thru town and on the far side of town 341 and 342 highways split. **Trucks, buses, and RV's are prohibited on 342 because of steep grade.** This road passes thru Gold Hill and Silver City, Nevada and then rejoins 341 just 5 miles down the hill.

The descent from Virginia City on 341 is **2-4% for 2 miles and then about 6% for 3 miles** to the junction with 342. There are 20 and 25 mph curves.

9 GOLCONDA SUMMIT elev. 5145'
(on I-80 between Winnemucca and Battle Mountain, NV)

Golconda Summit is about 30 miles west of Battle Mountain at milepost 200 on I-80. The westbound descent from the summit is almost 4 miles long and begins with 1/2 mile of 3% grade followed by **2 1/2 miles of 4-6% grade** and 1 mile of 2-3% grade.

The eastbound descent begins with about 4 miles of 3-4% grade and then a mile of 5% grade.

10 GOLDFIELD SUMMIT elev. 6078'
(on US 95 south of Goldfield, NV)

Goldfield Summit is about 1 3/4 miles south of Goldfield, Nevada. The descent southbound from the summit starts with about 1 1/2 miles of 5% grade. After that is 2-3% grade for several miles except for one section of 4% for 1/2 mile.

The northbound descent from the summit starts with about 1/2 mile of 5% grade, then 1/2 mile of 1-2% grade then about 4% for 3/4 mile into the town of Goldfield. After leaving town the grade is 1-2% for quite a few miles.

11 HICKISON SUMMIT elev. 6546'
(on US 50 east of Austin, NV)

Hickison Summit is about 23 1/2 miles east of Austin, Nevada. The eastbound descent from the summit is only 3% for 1 mile. The westbound descent is 6% for 1 mile then 2-3% for about 4 miles.

NEVADA

12 KINGSBERRY GRADE elev. 7334' (also known as DAGGETT SUMMIT)
(on Nevada Highway 207 south of Carson City, NV)

Daggett Summit is at the top of Kingsberry Grade about 11 1/4 miles west of the junction of Nevada State Highways 207 and 88.

The descent eastbound is steep and curvy with **6-8% grade for the first 5 1/2 miles. The next 2 1/2 miles alternate between about 4% and 6-7%.** The last 3 miles to the junction with State 88 are flat.

The westbound descent from the summit begins with a sign--**"9% grade 3 miles."** There are 20 mph curves. About a mile down from the summit a residential area is entered and 3 miles down from the summit is the junction with US 50.

13 MONTGOMERY PASS elev. 7132'
(on US 6 between Mount Montgomery, NV and the California state line.)

Montgomery Pass summit is about 8 miles east of the California state line on US 6. The descent westbound starts with about **2 1/2 miles of steady 6% grade.** The grade eases to about 4% for a mile then flattens out for two miles. The grade then goes back to 2-3% for several more miles into California.

The eastbound descent starts with almost **3 miles of 6% grade** then flattens out for about 3 miles. During the next 12 miles the road stairsteps down with most of the grade in the 3-4% range with 3 sections of 6% that are less than a mile long. The last few miles are 2-3%.

It is all good 2 lane road with 55 mph speed limit.

14 MT. AIRY SUMMIT elev. 6679' and NEW PASS SUMMIT elev. 6348'
(on US 50 west of Austin, NV)

All of the grades on Mt. Airy Summit and New Pass Summit are in the 1-3% range except for about **4 miles of 4-5% descent** on the west side of New Pass Summit.

15 MT. ROSE SUMMIT elev. 8911'
(on Nevada Highway 431 between Reno and Lake Tahoe, NV)

Heavy vehicles should use caution on this hill. The descents going both directions from the summit are long and steep.

The southbound descent from the summit of Mt. Rose is almost **steady 6-7% grade for 8 miles**. The speed limits are high enough to cause brakes to heat quickly if the driver isn't careful. There is a **runaway truck ramp 7 3/4 miles down the hill.** The ramp exits to the right and goes uphill but it is **very short.** Unfortunately, if your brakes are fading there is no good alternative because only 1/4 mile past the escape ramp there is a stop sign at a T-intersection. This is the junction with Nevada State Highway 28.

The northbound descent from the summit of Mt. Rose is about **16 miles of 5-7% grade** with several 20 mph hairpin turns and 20, 30, and 35 mph curves in the upper 7 or 8 miles of the hill. About 11 miles down the hill the road goes to 4 lane but the grade continues all the way to the junction of 431 and US 395. There is a stop light at this junction. *Be very careful on this hill. There are no escape ramps on this side.*

16 MURRAY SUMMIT elev. 7317'
(on US 6 west of Ely, NV)

Murray Summit is only about 4 1/2 miles west of the edge of Ely, Nevada. The eastbound descent towards Ely starts with about 1 1/2 miles of 3% grade. The next 3 miles into Ely vary from 4 to 6% but most of it is about 5%. The westbound descent from Murray Summit starts with about 2 miles of 5-6% grade then eases to about 2% for another mile or so.

17 NEW PASS SUMMIT--see MT. AIRY SUMMIT

18 OAK SPRINGS SUMMIT elev. 6237'
(on US 93 south of Caliente, NV)

Oak Springs Summit is about 10 miles south (actually west) of Caliente, Nevada. The northbound descent toward Caliente is about 7 1/2 miles of variable grade. The first 3 miles are mostly 3% or less grade with 2 short sections of 4-5%. The next **4 1/2 miles** are steeper with **4-6% grades** and 50 mph curves.

The descent southbound from the summit starts with about **3 miles of 4-5% grade**. After that the road stairsteps down for about 2 1/2 miles with a grade that might average 4%.

19 PAHROC SUMMIT elev. 4945'
(on US 93 south (actually west) of Caliente, NV)

Pahroc Summit is not marked and therefore a little bit difficult to pinpoint but it is about 10-12 miles east of the junction of US 93 and Nevada State Highway 375. Most of this 10-12 miles is a 3-4% descent going west with about 1 1/2 miles of 5-6% grade near the bottom. The grade eases back to 3-4% before reaching the junction.

There is little descent to the east of the summit toward Caliente.

20 PANCAKE SUMMIT elev. 6517'
(on US 50 between Eureka and Ely, NV)

Pancake Summit is about 13 miles west of Antelope Summit which is about midway between Eureka and Ely. The descent eastbound from the summit is only about **3 miles of 4-5% grade** and this includes some uphill when the road rolls up and down.

The westbound descent is about the same--3-4% grade and rolling hills for about 3 miles.

NEVADA

21 PEQUOP SUMMIT elev. 6967' and SILVER ZONE PASS elev. 5940'
(on I-80 between Wells and West Wendover, NV)

Pequop Summit is at milepost 373 1/2 east of Wells, Nevada. The descent westbound is mostly **4-6% grade for about 4 1/2 miles** with a couple of short sections where the grade eases to 1-2%. One section is about 1/2 mile long and the other is about 1/4 mile long.

The eastbound descent from Pequop Summit begins with almost **2 miles of 5-7% grade then 2 1/2 miles of 4-5% grade.** The grade then eases for several miles before beginning a long gradual climb to the summit of Silver Zone Pass. This climb is 6-7 miles of about 2% grade.

The eastbound descent from the summit of Silver Zone Pass is about 7 miles of grade that varies from 2% to 5%. The **4-5% lasts for about 3 1/2 miles** in the middle of the descent.

22 PINTO SUMMIT elev. 7376'
(on US 50 east of Eureka, NV)

Pinto Summit is about 4 miles east of Eureka. The eastbound descent is about 5 1/2 miles long with 1 mile of 5-6% at the top and 2 miles of 4-5% at the bottom with 2-4% grade in between.

The westbound descent starts with almost 2 miles of 6% and then eases to 2-4% the last 2 miles into Eureka.

23 REDLICH SUMMIT elev. 5053'
(on US 95 north of Coaldale, NV)

Redlich Summit is about 12 1/4 miles north of the junction of US 6 and US 95 at Coaldale. The 3 mile southbound descent from the summit is mostly about 2% grade with 2 short sections of 4-5% grade that are less than a mile each in length.

The northbound descent is 7 or 8 miles of mostly 2% with short sections of 3-4%.

24 ROBINSON SUMMIT elev. 7607'
(on US 50 west of Ely, NV)

Robinson Summit is about 16 1/2 miles west of Ely. It is a rather rough road. The descent eastbound toward Ely is only about 2 1/2 miles of 2-4% grade.

The westbound descent is 2-4% for about 5 1/2 miles. There is one section of 5% for less than 1/2 mile. This section is about 1 mile down from the summit.

25 SACRAMENTO PASS elev. 7145'
(on US 6/50 east of Ely, NV)

The summit of Sacramento Pass is about 20 miles east of the junction of US 6/50 and US 93.

The westbound descent starts with a truck warning sign--**"Steep grade-trucks use lower gear."** There is almost **5 miles of 4-6% grade**. The first 2 1/2 miles are about 6% grade and the next 2 1/2 miles are 4-5%. The first **4 miles** of the eastbound descent alternate between **5-6% and 3-4% grade.** The grade then eases and stairsteps down into the valley for about 7 miles.

NEVADA

26 SANDY SUMMIT elev. 6037' and BLACK ROCK SUMMIT
(on US 6 east of Blue Jay, NV)

Sandy Summit is about 8 miles east of Blue Jay on US 6. Black Rock Summit is somewhere east of Sandy Summit and since there are several hills in the area and Black Rock Summit is not marked the exact distance from Sandy Summit is a guess. The guess is 14 miles east of Sandy Summit.

The descent west from Sandy Summit is very gentle--about 1-3% for 8 miles. The descent east is also gentle with rolling grades of 1-3% for about 8 miles. There are some rolling hills for several miles before starting up what must be Black Rock Summit.

The climb up Black Rock is about 3% grade in stages for only a couple of miles. Then the descent to the east includes various grades from 3-6% for 4 1/2 miles. Most of the grade is about 4%.

27 SCOTT SUMMIT elev. 7267' and AUSTIN SUMMIT elev. 7484'
(on US 50 east of Austin, NV)

Scott Summit and Austin Summit are both just a few miles east of Austin, Nevada.

The eastbound descent from Scott Summit is about 6 miles of grade that varies from 2 to 6%. Most of the **6 miles is 4-6% grade** with 2 short sections of 2-3% grade and 35 mph curves.

The westbound descent is about **1 1/2 miles of 6%** grade with 45 mph curves. At this point the winding, **2 1/4 mile, 6%** climb to Austin Summit begins. There are some sharp 35 mph curves included.

The descent westbound from Austin Summit is also winding with 35 mph curves. The grade is **6-7% for almost 4 miles** which includes the whole 1 mile trip thru the town of Austin. At the junction of US 50 and Nevada State Highway 305 the grade eases for about 1/4 mile. Then it is back down at **4-6% for about 1 1/2 miles.** Several miles of 2-3% make a total descent of about 8 miles.

28 SILVER ZONE PASS--see PEQUOP SUMMIT

29 SPOONER SUMMIT elev. 7146'
(on US 50 between Carson City and Lake Tahoe, NV)

Spooner Summit is 9 miles west of the junction of US 395 and US 50. The road is 4 lane with 50 mph speed limit. **The 9 mile eastbound descent from the summit is almost all 5-6% grade.** The last couple of miles before the stop light at the junction have a couple of short stretches of lesser grade. **There is a runaway truck ramp 4 1/2 miles down from the summit.** There are a couple of warning signs before reaching it. *Use caution on this hill.*

The westbound descent from the summit begins with about **2 1/2 miles of 6-7% grade followed by 1 1/2 miles of 5%.** The grade then eases to 2-3% for about 1/2 mile. At this point the road is alongside Lake Tahoe and rolls up and down.

About 6 miles down from the summit there is a short **tunnel** with an arched top. **The vertical clearance on the right side is 12' 4".** The clearance in the center is marked **18' 6".**

OUNTAIN *VARIABLE ENGINE BRAKING*
TAMER **GAS**ᴬᴺᴅ**DIESEL** *SEE AD ON PAGE 3*

NEVADA

30 TONOPAH SUMMIT elev. 6256'
(on US 95 at Tonopah, NV)

Tonopah Summit is just south of US 6 on US 95 which means there are three descents from the summit--east and west on US 6 and south on US 95.

The westbound descent on US 6 is about 7 or 8 miles of 2-3% grade from the town of Tonopah. The eastbound descent on US 6 is about 5 miles of grade that varies from 2-4%.

Leaving the town of Tonopah southbound on US 95 takes you to Tonopah Summit just about 1/4 mile south of town. The descent goes down in stages. The first 2 miles are about 4% downhill then 3/4 mile flat grade. Then 1/2 mile of 4-5% grade followed by 1 mile of flat grade. Then 1 1/2 mile of 3-4% grade and 3/4 mile flat. The grade then goes to 1-3% for several miles.

31 TWIN SUMMITS--see EMIGRANT SUMMIT

32 WHITE HORSE PASS elev. 6025'
(on US Alt 93 south of West Wendover, NV)

White Horse Pass summit is about 29 miles south of West Wendover on US Alt. 93 highway. The northbound descent from the summit begins with about 8 miles of nearly level road and some rolling hills. Then there are 2 miles of 4-5% grade with short sections where the grade eases. The grade then goes to about 3-4% and continues to stairstep down for about 4 miles.

The southbound descent is about 4 miles of grade that varies from 2-4%.

33 See New Info on page 118

NEVADA

▲ —PASS OR STEEP GRADE LOCATIONS

NEW MEXICO

NEW MEXICO

1. APACHE PASS
2. BOBCAT PASS
3. CLOUDCROFT HILL
4. US 64 NEAR EAGLENEST
5. EMORY PASS
6. NEW MEXICO HIGHWAY 15
7. NEW MEXICO HIGHWAY 518
8. RATON PASS
9. SAN AUGUSTIN PASS
10. US 180 EAST OF LUNA
11. US 380 HONDO TO SAN ANTONIO
12. US 64 TRES PIEDRAS
    TO TIERRA AMARILLA
13. see New Info on page 119

1   **APACHE PASS** elev. 7591'
(on US 70 between Mescalero and Ruidoso, NM)

The summit of Apache Pass is at milepost 252 about 8 miles west of Ruidoso. The eastbound descent to Ruidoso starts with about 1 mile of 3-4% grade then 1 mile of 4-5% grade and then back to 3-4% for about 2 miles. The rest of the grade to Ruidoso is 2-3%.

The westbound descent begins with about 1 mile of 4-5% followed by about 5 miles of 3-4% grade. From this point the grade goes down in stages for about 10 or 11 miles including thru Mescalero and beyond. Most of the grade is fairly gradual.

2   **BOBCAT PASS** elev. 9820'
(on New Mexico Highway 38 between Eagle Nest and Red River, NM)

The summit of Bobcat Pass is about 12 1/2 miles north of Eagle Nest. The southbound descent is about **2 miles of 6-8% grade** with 25 to 45 mph curves followed by rolling hills of lesser grade to Eagle Nest. The northbound descent from the summit is about **4 miles of mostly 7-8% grade**. There are 30 and 35 mph curves and the grade continues right to the edge of the town of Red River.

NEW MEXICO

3   CLOUDCROFT HILL
(on US 82 between Alamogordo and Cloudcroft, NM)

The following signs appear as you leave Cloudcroft westbound--**"Warning truckers--steep downgrade--6% on US 82 *16 miles long* from Cloudcroft west--brake check area at Cloudcroft." "Trucks over 11 tons without retarder brakes prohibited on US 82 west of Cloudcroft."**

As you have probably guessed by now this is a nasty hill for westbounders. There is a 4315' drop in elevation in 16 miles. *This works out to an average of just over 5% for 16 miles.*

The descent towards Alamogordo begins right at the edge of Cloudcroft with signs saying--**"7% grade"** and **"6% grade next 16 miles." The grade varies between 6% and 7% almost the entire 16 miles.** There are only 2 or 3 places where the grade eases and these are short. **The truck speed limit is 35 mph.** There are 30 mph curves the first 3 miles and then 40 and 45 mph curves farther down.

There are *two runaway truck ramps* with plenty of warning signs before reaching them. The **first is about milepost 11 1/2** or almost 5 miles down the hill. The road curves to the right and the ramp exits right and goes uphill. The **second escape ramp is near milepost 5** or 11 miles down from the top of the hill. It exits to the right and goes uphill. There is a **tunnel** between the two escape ramps that is marked 17' 0" vertical clearance. Some of the road between the tunnel and the lower escape ramp is 3 lane but the rest is 2 lane. *Use extreme caution on this hill.*

The descent going east from Cloudcroft is very long and gradual except for a few short sections of 5-6% grade near Cloudcroft.

4   US 64 NEAR EAGLE NEST
(between Eagle Nest and Taos, NM)

There is a summit about 16 miles east of Taos on US 64 (milepost 272 1/2). The westbound descent towards Taos is very short with about 3/4 mile of 6% descent with a 15 mph curve at the bottom. The road from there to Taos is narrow with numerous 35 mph curves and rolling hills.

The eastbound descent from the summit begins with **2 miles of steady 6% grade** and constant 20 mph curves followed by about 2 miles of 4% grade and then rolling hills to Eagle Nest.

5   EMORY PASS elev. 8228'
(on New Mexico Highway 152 west of Kingston, NM)

Trucks over 12' 6" high are not permitted. *There are two bridges with 12' 8" vertical clearance just east of Kingston.* This road is almost constant curves from Kingston to the junction with State highway 35 which is 25 miles to the west. There are many 10, 15, 20, and 25 mph curves.

The summit of Emory Pass is about milepost 32. The eastbound descent is posted--**"Sharp curves--downgrade next 8 miles." Most of the 8 miles is about 6% grade** with 10 and 15 mph hairpin turns and 20 mph curves. The 8 miles of grade ends at Kingston where the road begins to straighten.

The westbound descent starts with about **4 miles of 6% grade** and 10 and 15 mph curves. The grade then eases and rolls up and down for a short distance.   The road works its way downhill for about another 10 miles with grades from 2 to 6% and the constant curves until you pass the junction with New Mexico Highway 35.

6 NEW MEXICO HIGHWAY 15
(between Silver City, NM and the Gila Cliff Dwellings National Monument)

About 5 miles north of Silver City is the town of Pinos Altos. Highway 15 is a good road to this point but there are signs posted for travel beyond Pinos Altos--**"Trailers over 20' unsafe beyond Pinos Altos"** and **"Caution--sharp curves next 18 miles"** and **"Caution no center stripe next 18 miles."**

The road is extremely narrow with many very sharp turns and little or no shoulder in places. The grade rolls up and down in short sections that are usually in the 4 to 7% range. Near the end of the 18 mile stretch there is a **descent of almost 3 miles with hairpin turns and 6 to 10% grades**. At the bottom of this grade is the junction with State 35 highway. (Highway 35 would be a few miles out of the way but a better road for large vehicles. There are a few very short grades of about 10% on highway 35 but as a whole it is a much better road than 15 up to this junction.)

Highway 15 improves greatly north of this junction as far as width and surface but it is still a mountain road with many curves and steep grades. **From milepost 26 (near the junction) to milepost 32 is almost all uphill at grades from 5% to 9 or 10%. (Of course, this means a descent of almost 6 miles on the return trip.)** After reaching the highest point (elev. 7440') the road rolls up and down for 1 1/2 miles with 7-10% grades and then there is a sign about milepost 32 1/2--**"Caution--downgrade next 5 miles." This descent is mostly 9-10% grade** with 20 mph curves and ends about 3 miles before you reach the Visitors Center at the Cliff Dwellings.

This can be a very difficult hill for large vehicles.

7 NEW MEXICO HIGHWAY 518
(between Holman and Taos, NM)

There are several stretches of steep grade on 518 between Holman and Taos. About 8 miles north of Holman is the top of one of these grades (about milepost 42.5). The descent south toward Holman is about **6 1/2 miles of 6-7% grade** with only one short stretch in the middle where the grade eases to 4-5%. The road is 2 lane with 50 mph curves near the top, 45 mph curves thru the middle and a 35 mph curve at the bottom of the grade. **Use caution on this hill.**

The descent northbound from the top of this grade is about 5 miles long but only the first 1/2 mile is 6-7% grade. The rest of the descent varies from 2-4% with 40 mph curves. After the grade flattens out the road runs alongside a river where trees and hills prevent the sun from reaching the pavement resulting in icy spots even in dry, sunny weather.

The junction of highways 518 and 75 is at milepost 57. Highway 75 stays with the river and 518 heads north toward Taos and immediately starts up a steep grade. The first 1 1/2 miles of the climb are about 6-7% grade. The next 2 miles vary from 2 to 5%. The hill tops out and starts down toward Taos at about 5-6% for almost 2 miles. There is a short uphill and then back down at grades from 4 to 7% over the next 2 1/2 miles. After this the road rolls up and down and opens up to 55 mph speed limit.

SCRATCH HERE

IF YOU *DON'T* SMELL BURNING BRAKES YOU MUST OWN A

MOUNTAIN TAMER

VARIABLE ENGINE BRAKING

GAS AND DIESEL

Also High Performance Torque Converters

DECEL-O-MATIC CORP
SEE AD ON PAGE 3

NEW MEXICO

8 RATON PASS elev. 7834'
(on I-25 north of Raton, NM)

The summit of Raton Pass is near the New Mexico--Colorado state line on I-25. The southbound descent towards Raton begins with about 1 1/2 miles of 6% grade followed by 1/2 mile of nearly flat road. Then there is another mile of 5-6% and 1 mile of 1-3% followed by 1 mile of 5-6% grade.

The northbound descent from the summit starts with 2 1/2 miles of 6% grade. The next 10 miles into Trinidad, Colorado are mostly 3-4% grade with several short 5-6% sections, each being about 1/4 mile long except for the last one. It is about 3/4 mile long as you drop into Trinidad.

9 SAN AUGUSTIN PASS elev. 5719'
(on US 70 east of Las Cruces, NM)

The summit of San Augustin Pass is about 13 1/2 miles east of the junction of I-25 and US 70 (milepost 164). The westbound descent toward Las Cruces starts with about **2 1/2 miles of 6% grade** including thru the town of Organ, New Mexico. After Organ there is about a mile of 3-4% grade for a total descent of about 4 miles.

The eastbound descent totals about 7 miles with the first 2 miles at 6% then 1/2 mile of 4% and then back to 6% for 1/2 mile. The remaining 4 miles are mostly 5% easing to 3% near the bottom. The road is all 4 lane.

There is a great deal of traffic on this road between Las Cruces and the White Sands Missle Range. It is very heavy at the morning and evening rush hours. The road is sometimes closed during missle tests.

10 US HIGHWAY 180
(east of Luna, NM)

There is a summit on US 180 about milepost 14 1/2. The westbound descent from this summit is about **3 miles of 6% grade** with 30 mph curves.

The eastbound descent is about **6 miles of grade that varies from 3 to 6%. Most of the grade is 5-6%** with 45 mph curves. This section of road has been rebuilt recently (as of fall 1993) and is in excellent shape. As of this writing some of the road west of here to the state line and much of the road east of this hill are still narrow and rough.

11 US HIGHWAY 380
(between Hondo and San Antonio, NM)

Some general information about US 380: There are several small mountain ranges scattered along this road. The grades between Hondo and Carrizozo are usually fairly gradual and the highway is mediocre. The grades between Carrizozo and Bingham are sometimes in the 5-6% range but not steady--they stairstep up and down--sometimes for 4 or 5 miles. The road is very poor between Carrizozo and Bingham. It is very narrow and rough. West of Bingham the road returns to mediocre and is almost flat except for the last few miles into San Antonio where the grade stairsteps down to the junction with I-25.

12 US HIGHWAY 64
(between Tres Piedras and Tierra Amarilla, NM)

This road is often closed during the winter months due to deep snowdrifts. There are many short, steep hills all the way across this section of highway. There are two areas where they are more lengthy.

There is an eastbound descent from milepost 200 1/2 to milepost 208 1/2. The grade starts down at about 3% for a couple of miles and then is **5-6% for about 6 miles** with only a couple of short breaks in the grade. It is all 2 lane with 35 mph curves.

The other lengthy grade is a westbound descent from milepost 193 to milepost 185. The **first 5 miles are mostly 6% grade** with 30 mph curves. The grade eases to about 4% for a couple of miles and then 3% for several miles.

13 see New Info on page 119

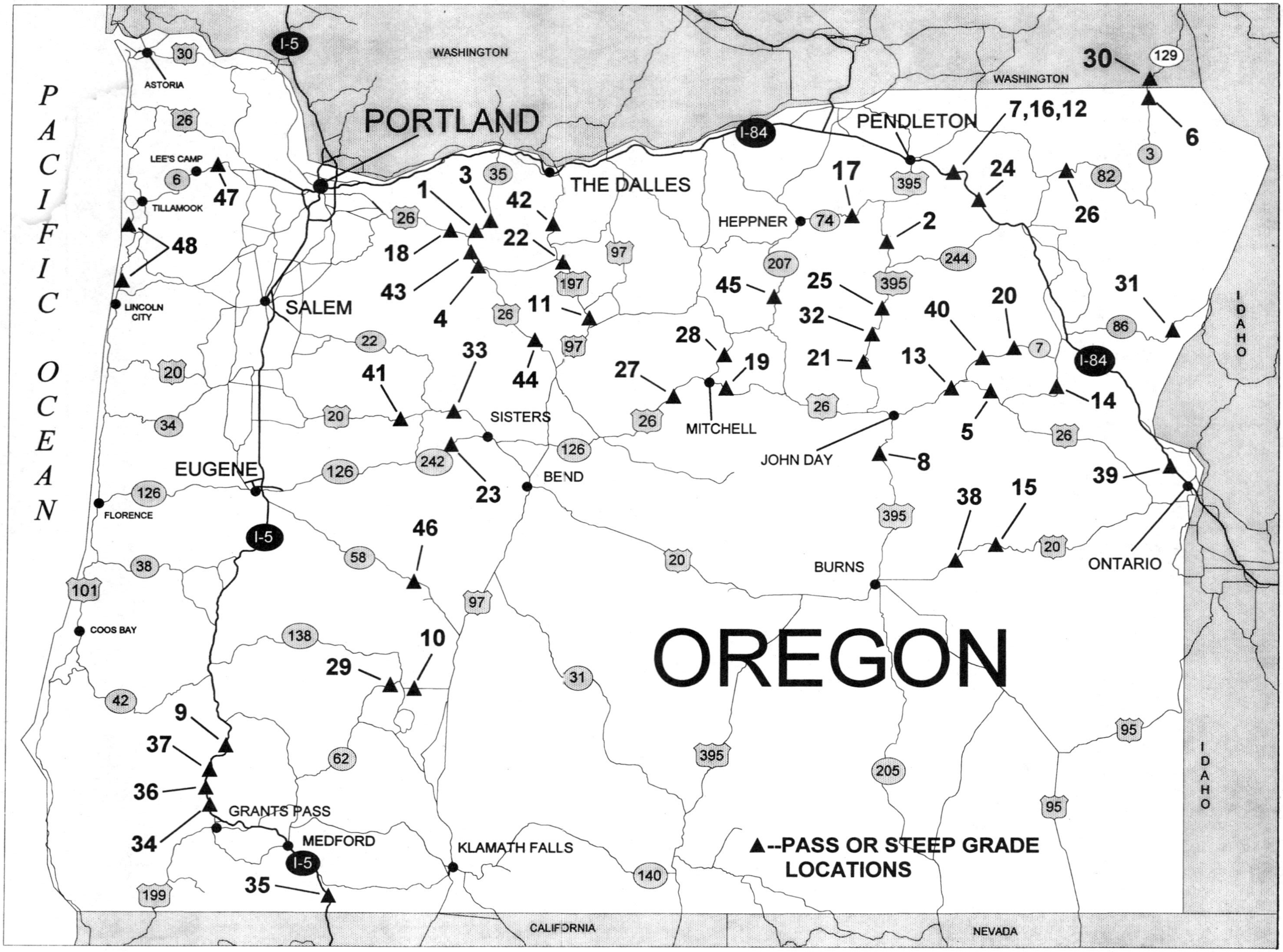

MapInfo® is the registered trademark of MapInfo Corporation, Troy, New York.

OREGON

1. BARLOW PASS
2. BATTLE MOUNTAIN SUMMIT
3. BENNETT PASS
   (see BARLOW PASS)
4. BLUE BOX PASS
   (see GOVERNMENT CAMP SUMMIT)
5. BLUE MOUNTAIN PASS
6. BUFORD GRADE *
7. CABBAGE HILL
8. CANYON CITY HILL
9. CANYON CREEK PASS
   (see SEXTON MOUNTAIN PASS)
10. CASCADE MOUNTAIN PASS
11. COW CANYON GRADE
12. DEADMAN'S PASS
    (see CABBAGE HILL)
13. DIXIE PASS
14. DOOLEY MOUNTAIN SUMMIT
15. DRINKWATER PASS
16. EMIGRANT HILL
    (see CABBAGE HILL)
17. FRANKLIN HILL SUMMIT
18. GOVERNMENT CAMP SUMMIT
19. KEYES CREEK SUMMIT
20. LARCH SUMMIT
21. LONG CREEK MOUNTAIN SUMMIT
22. MAUPIN HILL
    (see COW CANYON GRADE)
23. McKENZIE PASS
24. MEACHAM SUMMIT
    (see CABBAGE HILL)
25. MEADOW BROOK SUMMIT
26. MINAM HILL SUMMIT
27. OCHOCO PASS
28. OREGON HIGHWAY 207
29. OREGON HIGHWAY 230
30. RATTLESNAKE GRADE
    (see BUFORD GRADE)
31. RICHLAND HILL
32. RITTER BUTTE SUMMIT
    (see LONG CREEK MOUNTAIN SUMMIT)
33. SANTIAM PASS
34. SEXTON MOUNTAIN PASS
35. SISKIYOU SUMMIT **
36. SMITH HILL SUMMIT
    (see SEXTON MOUNTAIN PASS)
37. STAGE ROAD PASS
    (see SEXTON MOUNTAIN PASS)
38. STINKINGWATER PASS
    (see DRINKWATER PASS)
39. THREE MILE HILL
40. TIPTON SUMMIT
41. TOMBSTONE SUMMIT
42. TYGH RIDGE SUMMIT
    (see COW CANYON GRADE)
43. WAPINITIA PASS
    (see GOVERNMENT CAMP SUMMIT)
44. WARM SPRINGS GRADE
    (see GOVERNMENT CAMP SUMMIT)
45. WETMORE SUMMIT
    (see OREGON HIGHWAY 207)
46. WILLAMETTE PASS
47 & 48 see New Info on page 119

* In both Washington and Oregon directories.
** In both Oregon and California directories.

GEAR VENDORS UNDER/OVERDRIVE™
MORE POWER... BETTER ECONOMY.
See ad on Page 29

OREGON

1   **BARLOW PASS** elev. 4155' and **BENNETT PASS** elev. 4670'
(on Oregon Highway 35 south of Hood River, OR)

Starting from the junction of State highway 35 and US 26 and heading north on State 35 it is only about **2 miles of 5-6% climb** before reaching the summit of Barlow Pass.

The descent on the northbound side of Barlow Pass is about 1 mile of 4-5% grade. Then the climb to the summit of Bennett Pass begins. This climb is only about 3 miles of rolling highway with some short stretches of 5-6% uphill grade.

From the summit of Bennett Pass the northbound descent starts with about **1 mile of 4-5% grade followed by about 3 1/2 miles of 5-6% grade.** Then there is a rolling descent with 3-4% grades for several miles.

2   **BATTLE MOUNTAIN SUMMIT** elev. 4270'
(on US 395 north of Ukiah, OR)

Battle Mountain Summit has about 2 miles of 4-6% grade on both sides of the summit with 25, 30, and 35 mph curves. On the northbound side, after the first 2 miles of 4-6%, there is a very long, gradual descent past the junction of US 395 and State 74 highway.

3   **BENNETT PASS**--see BARLOW PASS

4   **BLUE BOX PASS**--see GOVERNMENT CAMP SUMMIT

5   **BLUE MOUNTAIN PASS** elev. 5109'
(on US 26 between Unity and Austin Junction, OR)

There are several passes or summits named Blue Mountain in Oregon. This one is on US 26 at milepost 199 between Unity and Austin Junction.

The westbound descent is about 3 1/2 miles in length. The first 1 1/2 miles are about 5-6% grade with 35 and 40 mph curves. The grade eases over the next 2 miles to about 2-4%.

The eastbound descent is about **4 miles of 4-5% grade.**

6 BUFORD GRADE
(on Oregon Highway 3 north of Enterprise, OR)
RATTLESNAKE GRADE
(on Washington Highway 129 south of Clarkston, WA)

The Grande Ronde River flows near the Washington-Oregon border on the eastern edge of these states. Washington State Highway 129 crosses the river and a few miles later crosses the state line where it becomes Oregon State Highway 3.

There are long, steep descents to the river from both north and south. The descent on the Washington side is called Rattlesnake Grade. The descent on the Oregon side is called Buford Grade.

The descent from the north down Rattlesnake Grade begins about milepost 14 1/2. **There is no steep grade warning.** There is a sign stating--**"25 mph curves next 9 miles."** The first mile is about 3-4% grade. The next **9 miles are about 6%** with constant 20, 25, and 30 mph curves all the way down.

The descent from the south down Buford Grade also begins with about 1 mile of 3-4% grade and then about **9 1/2 miles of 6%** and then 1/2 mile of 3-4% before reaching the river. There are 20, 25, and 30 mph curves all the way to the bottom. The Oregon-Washington state line is crossed about 6 miles down the hill. ***Use caution on these descents.***

It is customary for logging trucks and other local truckers to use the CB radio to announce their position on these grades. They call out which milepost they're passing, which hill they're on, whether they are going up or down, and if they are loaded or empty. The road is very narrow and winding so you usually can't see very far ahead. Some of the curves are too tight for two trucks to get by each other so the announcement of position helps avoid problems.

OREGON

7 CABBAGE HILL
EMIGRANT HILL
DEADMAN'S PASS
MEACHAM SUMMIT
(all on I-84 east of Pendleton, OR)

Cabbage Hill is the popular name for what is correctly called Emigrant Hill, but you may not see either name on your map. What you might see is Deadman's Pass, which is a rest area about 5 miles east of Cabbage Hill, or you might see Meacham Summit which is a few miles east of Deadman's Pass. This hill has a reputation among truckers for being a dangerous descent, partly due to the length and grade and partly due to the possibility of very nasty weather in the winter.

On Cabbage Hill the eastbound and westbound lanes of I-84 are separated and have different grades and speed limits. There follows a description of the eastbound climb and the westbound descent.

The eastbound climb starts with a chain up area at milepost 216 1/2. At about milepost 217 the grade starts up at about 2%. At milepost 218 it goes to 3% and at 218 1/2 to 4-5%. The next **6 miles are 5-6% uphill** with 40, 45, and 50 mph curves. There is another chain up area at milepost 221. At milepost 225 the grade eases to about 3% and continues until milepost 229. **This is a total pull of about 12 miles.** This can be a severe test on engine cooling systems in the summer.

The westbound descent of Cabbage Hill begins with a warning sign--**"6 miles of 6% downgrade ahead."** This warning is repeated several times. At milepost 227 there is a sign--**"weigh station and brake test area--all trucks over 20,000 lbs. next right."** About milepost 226 1/2 there is another sign with the following information:

5 axles or more:

weight (lbs.)	speed limit
60,000 to 65,000	37 mph
65,000 to 70,000	26 mph
70,000 to 75,000	22 mph
75,000 to 80,000	18 mph

These speed limits are good guidelines on any long, steep descent.

The 6% grade starts near milepost 224 1/2. About 1/2 mile down there is a sign advising of **two escape ramps. The first is at milepost 222 and the second is at milepost 220.** Both of these exit to the right and are upsloping ramps. There is about 1 1/2 miles of 6% grade after the second escape ramp. The total descent is about 6 miles of 6% grade.

8 CANYON CITY HILL elev. 5152'
(on US 395 south of Canyon City, OR)

The summit of this hill is about 13 1/2 miles south of Canyon City. The descent is northbound and starts about milepost 15 1/2. It is about **6% for 4 1/2 miles** with 25, 30, and 40 mph curves. The curves are almost continuous.

OREGON

9 CANYON CREEK PASS--see SEXTON MOUNTAIN PASS

10 **CASCADE MOUNTAIN PASS** elev. 5925'
(on Oregon Highway 138 on the north edge of Crater Lake National Park, OR)
    The westbound descent from the summit of Cascade Mountain Pass is very gradual. Most of the grade is 2-3% or sometimes 4%. There are several stretches of 5-6% but they only last 1/2 to 1 mile. The descent is spread over many miles. The 2 and 3% grades continue for over 30 miles to the west. There are some 4-5% hills to descend as you approach Roseburg but they are not long.
    The eastbound descent lasts about 6 miles but most of it is gradual. The road is straight as an arrow and you can see the whole descent ahead of you. There are two sections of 6% grade--one is about 3/10 mile long and the other is about 8/10 mile long. The rest is 2-4%.

11 **COW CANYON GRADE**
(on US 97 north of Willowdale, OR)
MAUPIN HILL
(on US 197 at Maupin, OR)
TYGH RIDGE SUMMIT
(on US 197 north of Tygh Valley, OR)
    Between Willowdale, Oregon and the junction of US 97 and US 197 to the north, is Cow Canyon.
    The southbound descent on US 97 into Cow Canyon is about 6 miles in length. It starts with **2 miles of 4% followed by 3 miles of 5-6% and another mile of 4% near the bottom.** US 97 is 2 lane with a passing lane during the steeper parts of the grade.
    Farther north on US 197 at about milepost 54 the descent into the town of Maupin begins. There is a sign for northbound traffic--**"Steep grade next 5 miles."** The first mile is about 5-6% and then the grade eases to 4-5%. About 2 miles down from the sign the road begins stairstepping down for another 3 miles to milepost 48 where there is another sign--**"6% grade next 2 miles."** This is the last 2 miles into Maupin and there are 20, 25, and 30 mph curves and the grade doesn't ease until you have entered town.
    Leaving Maupin northbound there are about **3 miles of 5-6% uphill grade** until reaching the junction of US 197 and Oregon State highway 216. There are 20 and 25 mph curves.
    Tygh Ridge Summit is south of The Dalles and north of Tygh Valley on US 197. The northbound descent from the summit is about **2 miles of 6% grade**. The southbound descent is about 5 1/2 miles in length. The first **4 1/2 miles are steady 6-7% grade** followed by about 1 mile of 3-4% grade.

12 DEADMAN'S PASS--see CABBAGE HILL

Instant Power You can FEEL! Improves Acceleration, Hill Climbing & Passing!

GIBSON PERFORMANCE EXHAUST SYSTEMS
Complete Exhaust Systems...from Headers to Stainless Steel tip
TRUCKS and MOTORHOMES! • Lowest Price/Highest Quality
Aluminized & Stainless Bolt-on Kits • 50 State Legal • Lifetime Warranty
GIBSON PERFORMANCE EXHAUST SYSTEMS

714/528-3044 • FREE CATALOG • 800/528-3044

OREGON

13 DIXIE PASS elev. 5279'
(on US 26 between Prairie City and Austin Junction, OR)

Dixie Pass is about milepost 184 on US 26 highway. The eastbound descent from the summit of Dixie Pass is about 5 miles in length. The first 1 1/2 miles are in the 4-6% range. The grade eases to 2-4% over the last 3 1/2 miles. There are 40 mph curves on this pass.

The westbound descent from the summit is about 7 miles in length. Most of this descent is in the **5-6%** range but there are three sections where the grade flattens out for 1/2 to 1 mile.

US 26 highway is being widened on the west side of Dixie Pass in the fall of 1993.

14 DOOLEY MOUNTAIN SUMMIT elev. 5392'
(on Oregon Highway 245 south of Baker City, OR)

Dooley Mountain Summit is at milepost 29 on State 245 south of Baker City. This mountain road is narrow and winding.

The descent northbound begins with a warning sign--**"downgrade next 5 miles."** The grade alternates between **4 and 6%** for the entire descent. It is closer to **6 miles in length**. The 20 mph curves are continuous all the way down.

The southbound descent also begins with a warning sign--**"downgrade next 5 miles."** This side of the hill is **5-6% for almost 8 miles**. The continuous 25 mph curves last almost 5 miles. Then, after a couple of **15 mph hairpin turns**, the road opens up but the grade remains about 5-6% for 2 more miles.

15 DRINKWATER PASS elev. 4212' and STINKINGWATER PASS elev. 4848'
(on US 20 west of Juntura, OR)

The summit of Drinkwater Pass is at milepost 177 1/2. The descent westbound is **6% for 3 miles**. The descent eastbound is 5% for 1 mile.

The summit of Stinkingwater Pass is at milepost 161 on US 20 west of Drinkwater Pass and east of Buchanan, Oregon. The eastbound descent is marked--**"Steep grade next 5 miles." The grade is mostly 5-6% for the 5 miles.** The westbound descent from the summit starts with about 2 1/2 miles of rolling grade in the 3-4% range. At milepost 158 there is a steep grade sign with no details. It is **4-6%** downhill from there for about **3 1/2 miles** into Buchanan.

16 EMIGRANT HILL--see CABBAGE HILL

17 FRANKLIN HILL SUMMIT elev. 3456'
(on Oregon Highway 74 east of Heppner, OR)

The Franklin Hill Summit is at milepost 64 on State highway 74. This is a narrow two lane road. From the summit eastbound the first 3 1/2 miles are rolling hills and not too steep. The next **3 1/2 miles are about 5%** descent with 35 and 40 mph curves.

Going west from the summit the grade is about **6% for 4 miles** with several 20 mph hairpin turns and numerous 25, 30, and 35 mph curves.

OREGON

18 GOVERNMENT CAMP SUMMIT
WAPINITIA PASS elev. 3949'
BLUE BOX PASS elev. 4024'
WARM SPRINGS GRADE
(all on US 26 east of Portland, OR)

All of these grades are on US 26 between Portland and Madras, Oregon.

The Government Camp Summit is about 2 miles west of the junction of Oregon State highway 35 and US 26. The westbound descent from the summit begins with about 2 miles of 3% grade during which there are numerous warnings about the grade ahead. The signs warn--**"6% grade next 5 miles"** and **"Warning--long steep downgrade ahead."** There is a brake check pulloff. Much of the descent is 3 lane or 4 lane road with 35 mph curves. ***There is a runaway truck ramp 2 1/2 miles down from the beginning of the 6% grade.*** There are several warning signs as you approach the ramp.

The eastbound descent is about 3 1/2 miles of mostly 3-4% grade. There is one section of 6-7% for about 1/2 mile before the junction of US 26 and State 35 highways.

At the end of the 3 1/2 miles descent the climb to the summits of Wapinitia Pass and Blue Box Pass begins. About 3 1/4 miles of climbing at 3-6% brings you to Wapinitia Pass summit and about one mile of mild grade later you are at the summit of Blue Box Pass.

The eastbound descent from the summit of Blue Box Pass is rolling hills with some short 5-6% sections, but mostly 2-4% grades with 2 and 3 lane road and 45 mph curves.

Farther east on US 26 at about milepost 99 the eastbound descent into Warm Springs begins. It is about **4 1/2 miles of 5-6% grade.** The westbound descent into Warm Springs is about 3-4% for the first mile and then **5-6% for about 2 1/4 miles** before easing to **about 4% the last 2 miles.**

19 KEYES CREEK SUMMIT elev. 4382'
(on US 26 east of Mitchell, OR)

Keyes Creek Summit is about milepost 73 on US 26, or about 6 miles east of Mitchell, Oregon. There is very little descent on the east side of the summit. There are some short 4% hills.

There is a brake check pullout at the summit for westbound traffic. The descent on the west side is about **3 1/2 miles of 6% grade, then 1 mile of about 4%, then back to 5-6% for another mile and then about 4% on into Mitchell.** The speed limit is mostly 55 mph with a 45 mph curve 1/2 mile before arriving at the edge of Mitchell.

20 LARCH SUMMIT elev. 5082'
(on Oregon Highway 7 north of Austin, OR)

Larch Summit is at milepost 21 1/2 on State highway 7 north of Austin. The southbound descent is about 1 mile of 5-6% followed by 1/2 mile of 3-4%. There are 35 mph curves.

The northbound descent is **3 miles of 5-6% grade** with 30, 35, and 40 mph curves.

OREGON

21 LONG CREEK MOUNTAIN SUMMIT elev. 5075'
(on US 395 south of Long Creek, OR)
RITTER BUTTE SUMMIT elev. 3993'
(on US 395 north of Long Creek, OR)

The southbound descent from Long Creek Mountain Summit is about **2 1/2 miles of 6% grade** with 45 mph curves. At the bottom of the grade is the small town of Fox, Oregon.

The northbound descent is **4 miles of steady 6% grade** with 30, 35, and 40 mph curves. At the bottom of the hill is the town of Long Creek with 35 mph speed limit and a 25 mph school zone.

North of Long Creek there is a series of rolling hills with fairly steep grades but none of them are very long. They continue to the top of Ritter Butte Summit, near milepost 81.

The north side of Ritter Butte Summit is a **4 mile 5-6% descent** with 35 and 45 mph curves. The south side of Ritter Butte Summit is the series of rolling hills described above.

22 MAUPIN HILL--see COW CANYON GRADE

23 McKENZIE PASS elev. 5325'
(on Oregon Highway 242 west of Sisters, OR)

This road is closed in winter. Trailer traffic is not recommended. Vehicles over 50' prohibited. Extremely narrow and winding--especially on west side of the pass.

The "highway" on the west side of this pass is so narrow that in many places a regular sized vehicle such as a pickup or van will be over the center line. The hairpin turns are very tight. There are vertical rocks on the edge of the road in places. A small motor home might make it over this pass but there is a risk of damage. If you want to see the lava fields at the top of the mountain go up and down the east side. It is wider and straighter and the grade is less steep.

Truckers--save yourself a lot of time and headache--go around.

The westbound descent from the Lava Observatory at the summit is about **18 miles of 5-6% grade.** There are many 15 and 20 mph hairpin turns and many more 15, 20, and 25 mph curves.

The eastbound descent is rolling hills for the first 3 1/2 miles. Over the next **4 miles** the downhill grade varies from **4 to 6%** and then eases to 1-2% for the rest of the way into Sisters.

24 MEACHAM SUMMIT--see CABBAGE HILL

25 MEADOW BROOK SUMMIT elev. 4127'
(on US 395 south of Ukiah and Dale, OR)

The summit of Meadow Brook Pass is at milepost 71 1/2. The southbound descent from the summit is **4-5% for almost 3 miles** with 35 mph curves. After 3 miles the grade eases to about 3% for 2 more miles into Ritter Junction.

The northbound descent is about **7 1/2 miles of grade that varies from 3% to 5%** with 25, 35, and 40 mph curves. The grade flattens out about a mile after passing thru Dale, Oregon.

OREGON

26 MINAM HILL SUMMIT elev. 3650'
(on Oregon Highway 82 between Elgin and Minam, OR)

Minam Hill Summit is about 8 miles east of Elgin and 6 miles west of Minam, Oregon. The descent westbound to Elgin is rolling hills with 3, 4, and 5% grades. The last **2 miles** into Elgin are **steady 5% downhill.**

The eastbound descent begins with a warning sign--**"Steep grade next 4 miles." The grade is 4-6%** with 30 and 40 mph curves and lasts the promised 4 miles. This side of the hill is under construction in the fall of 1993 and will probably be wider and have more 3 lane.

27 OCHOCO PASS elev. 4722'
(on US 26 west of Mitchell, OR)

The summit of Ochoco Pass is at milepost 50 on US 26 about 16 miles west of Mitchell. The eastbound descent of Ochoco Pass has some short 5-6% hills near the top with stretches of 2-3% in between. About 3 miles down from the summit a **3 1/2 mile section of 5-6%** begins. After that the grade eases back to 3-4% and begins to roll again. There are 35, 40, and 45 mph curves all the way down.

The westbound descent is only a couple of miles of rolling 4 and 5% grade.

28 OREGON HIGHWAY 207 including WETMORE SUMMIT
(between Heppner and Mitchell, OR)

Going south out of Heppner on 206/207 there is a **3 mile climb at 5-6%** with 25 and 35 mph curves. The road is 2 lane. After topping the hill the road is fairly flat for about 3 miles. Then it's **downhill** for about **3 1/2 miles at 5%** with 40 mph curves. The grade bottoms out at Ruggs, Oregon where 206 and 207 separate.

South of Ruggs, at about milepost 5 on highway 207 southbound, a **3 1/2 mile 5% climb** begins with 30 and 35 mph curves. At the top of the climb there is a 1/2 mile dip into and out of Hardman, Oregon. Then a **2 1/2 mile 6% descent** begins with 25 and 45 mph curves. The descent bottoms out about milepost 11.

Wetmore Summit is at milepost 27 on highway 207 north of Spray, Oregon. The descent northbound is rolling hills or almost flat road to milepost 22. Then the descending grade varies from 2% to 5% over the next 5 or 6 miles. The southbound descent is **4-5% for 2 1/2 miles then 5-6% for about 4 miles.** At this point the grade bottoms out and climbs at 4-6% for about 1 mile. Then there is another **6 miles of 4-6% downhill grade** to the junction of highways 207 and 19. During the upper part of this descent there are 20 mph hairpin turns and 20, 25, and 30 mph curves. The lower part of the descent has 25, 30, and 35 mph curves. It is all 2 lane highway.

Between Service Creek and Mitchell, Oregon there are climbs and descents in the **5-6%** range that can be **several miles long**. There is at least one short hill in the **8-9%** range. It is near milepost 7 1/2 and has a 45 mph curve at the bottom of it. It is a descent for southbound traffic.

OREGON

29 OREGON HIGHWAY 230
(north of Crater Lake National Park, OR)

This summit (elev. 5415') is about 4 miles west of the junction of State highway 138 and State highway 230 just north of Crater Lake National Park. The descent eastbound towards the junction is rolling hills with grades in the 2-3% range.

The descent westbound starts with rolling hills and 3% grades for about 2 miles. **The next 3 miles of grade varies from 4-6%, then 3 miles of 2-3%, then 1 mile of 6%** with 35 mph curves. The grade eases for about 4 miles before entering another series of 35 mph curves and 6% descent. This series of curves seems to appear rather suddenly and without much warning. The grade only lasts about 1/2 mile and then the road begins to roll up and down.

State highway 230 soon turns into State 62 and about 24 miles west of this change there is a **6% grade for 2 miles**. This hill is near milepost 31.

30 RATTLESNAKE GRADE--see BUFORD GRADE

31 RICHLAND HILL elev. 3653'
(on Oregon Highway 86 between Richland and Halfway, OR)

Going east from the summit of Richland Hill the first **2 miles are 7% downhill grade** with 30 and 35 mph curves. The grade then eases to 3-4% for the remaining 2 1/4 miles into Halfway except for two very short sections of 6% grade.

The westbound descent from the summit of Richland Hill begins with about a mile of rolling hills and then a sign saying--**"7% grade next 3 miles."** The next 3 miles are indeed about 7% with 30, 35, and 40 mph curves. The next 1 1/2 miles are 3-5% grade and you arrive in Richland.

32 RITTER BUTTE SUMMIT--see LONG CREEK MOUNTAIN SUMMIT

33 SANTIAM PASS elev. 4817'
(on US 20/Oregon 126 west of Sisters, OR)

The summit of Santiam Pass is at milepost 81 on combined highway US 20 and Oregon Highway 126. The eastbound descent is **3 and 4% for the first 3 miles** with some 45 mph curves. **The next 2 1/2 miles are 5% grade**. After that the grade varies from almost flat to 3-4% for several miles.

The westbound descent begins with mild grade for the first mile and several warning signs--**"Steep grade--trucks use lower gear"** and **"Downgrade next 4 1/2 miles."** There is a brake check area just before the westbound descent begins about 1 mile west of the summit. The descent begins with about **2 1/2 miles of 5-6% grade**. The grade eases for about 1 mile and then starts uphill at 4-5% for 3/4 mile and then back down at 5-6% for a mile to the junction with Oregon State Highway 22.

If you continue on State 126 toward Eugene you will find mostly rolling hills, some fairly steep but not too long, until you reach milepost 7 1/2. At this point (westbound) a descent begins at **5-6% for 2 1/2 miles** followed by 1 1/2 miles of 3-4%.

If you take State highway 22 toward Salem the grade is mostly rolling with some steep but short hills. Between milepost 77 and milepost 75 1/2 there is a **2 1/2 mile 5-6% descent**. Also, at Detroit Dam there is a **6% descent for 1 1/2 miles** (milepost 43).

OREGON

34 SEXTON MOUNTAIN PASS elev. 1960'
SMITH HILL SUMMIT elev. 1730'
STAGE ROAD PASS elev. 1830'
CANYON CREEK PASS elev. 2020'
(all on Interstate 5 between Roseburg and Grants Pass, OR)

Sexton Mountain Pass--summit milepost 69.
3 miles of 6% on both sides of the summit.
50 and 55 mph curves.

Smith Hill Summit--summit at milepost 74.
2 miles of 6% on both sides of the summit.
45 and 50 mph curves.

Stage Road Pass--summit milepost 80.
2 miles of 4-5% on the south side.
1 1/2 miles of 6% on the north side.

Canyon Creek Pass--summit milepost 90.
2 miles of 5-6% on the south side.
3 miles of 6% on the north side

35 SISKIYOU SUMMIT elev. 4310'
(on I-5 just north of the Oregon-California state line)

Chains may be required on this hill in winter. Siskiyou Summit is about milepost 4 1/2 on the Oregon side of the state line. ***There are two escape ramps on the north side of the hill.*** The descent is **7 miles of 6% on both sides of the hill.**

The northbound descent is a **steady 6% grade** with 55 mph truck speed limit and 50 mph curves. ***The first runaway truck ramp is at milepost 6.2 and the second is at milepost 9.4.*** They are 1 3/4 and 5 miles down from the summit. **Use caution on this hill.**

The southbound descent starts down at **6%**. About **2 1/4 miles** down from the summit the grade eases to about **4% for 1 1/2 miles**. It then goes back to **6% for another 1 1/2 miles** and then eases again for 1 1/4 miles. Then it's back downhill at **6% for 1 1/2 miles**. At this point there is a sign--**"4% grade next 2 miles."** Two miles farther down the hill there is an inspection station--all vehicles must stop. "Brakeless trucks use left lane."

About 4 miles south of the inspection station there is a **1 1/2 mile 6% descent and then a 4 mile 6% climb and then a 3 mile 5% descent.**

There is also a **3 mile 5% southbound descent** that bottoms out at Dunsmuir, California.

36 SMITH HILL SUMMIT--see SEXTON MOUNTAIN PASS

37 STAGE ROAD PASS--see SEXTON MOUNTAIN PASS

38 STINKINGWATER PASS--see DRINKWATER PASS

MOUNTAIN TAMER — *VARIABLE ENGINE BRAKING* **GAS**ᴬᴺᴅ**DIESEL** *SEE AD ON PAGE 3*

OREGON

39 THREE MILE HILL
(on I-84 west of Ontario, OR)

The summit of Three Mile Hill is at milepost 359 on I-84 west of Ontario, Oregon. For westbound traffic there is a warning sign--**"Steep grade next 3 miles."** The 3 miles of descent are in the **5-6% range**. For those traveling eastbound from the summit of Three Mile Hill the next 14 miles are up and down all the way to Ontario. There are 5 and 6% grades both up and down but they only last from 1/2 to 1 3/4 miles. The last 7 miles into Ontario are mostly 3-4% hills.

40 TIPTON SUMMIT elev. 5124'
(on Oregon Highway 7 north of Austin, OR)

Tipton Summit is about milepost 7 1/2 on State highway 7 north of Austin. The southbound descent starts with about 3/4 mile of 3% grade and then goes to **5-6% for 1 mile. After that the grade is 4-5% for about 3 miles.**

The northbound descent begins with about 1 mile of fairly flat road. During this mile there is a sign--**"Steep grade--6%."** The first mile after the sign is about 4-5% and then there is about **2 miles of 6% grade** with 35 and 40 mph curves.

41 TOMBSTONE SUMMIT elev. 4236'
(on US 20 east of Sweet Home, OR)

Tombstone Summit is at milepost 63 1/2 on US 20 east of Sweet Home. The westbound descent from the summit begins with a truck warning sign--**"6% grade next 11 miles."** *The sign is accurate.* **The grade is steady** with constant 25, 30, and 35 mph curves and the road is rough 2 lane. The grade eases to about 3% just before reaching Upper Soda and continues for several miles at 3%.

The eastbound descent starts with about **3 miles of 5-6% grade** and then rolling hills to the junction with State highway 126.

42 TYGH RIDGE SUMMIT--see COW CANYON GRADE

43 WAPANITIA PASS--see GOVERNMENT CAMP SUMMIT

44 WARM SPRINGS GRADE--see GOVERNMENT CAMP SUMMIT

45 WETMORE SUMMIT--see OREGON STATE HIGHWAY 207

OREGON

46 WILLAMETTE PASS elev. 5128'
(on Oregon Highway 58 east of Oakridge, OR)

The summit of Willamette Pass is at milepost 62 on State highway 58.

The eastbound descent from the summit starts with about 1 1/2 miles of 4-5% grade and then eases to about 3% for 1/2 mile. The next 10 or 11 miles are rolling hills with about 3% grade both uphill and down. The last several miles before reaching the junction with US 97 are a series of steeper hills, both uphill and down, but they are not very long.

Going westbound over the summit there are warning signs--**"Warning--6% downgrade ahead"** and **"Truck brake check area ahead"** and **"Downgrade next 13 miles."** The first **5 miles** of descent are in the **4-5%** range and there are several short stretches where the grade eases and one half mile stretch where the grade is 5-6%. There are 40 and 45 mph curves.

Five miles down from the summit there are more warning signs--**"Warning--downgrade ahead"** and **"Downgrade next 5 miles--6%."** The grade goes to 6% and about 1/2 mile down the hill from these warning signs there is a 1/4 mile long **tunnel** with an arched opening that is marked **13' 8" vertical clearance along the right side.** The tunnel curves gradually and the grade continues at about 6% thru it. There is obviously no sun on the pavement in the tunnel so it is possible the tunnel could be slick when the road outside is not.

Just downhill from the tunnel is a sign--**"Warning truckers--maximum grade begins 1 mile."** The grade eases slightly for a short distance and then goes to a **steady 6%** with many 45 mph curves. ***There are two runaway truck ramps, the first at milepost 54 and the second at 52 1/2.*** There are several warning signs before each ramp. In both cases the road makes a 45 mph curve to the left and the ramp goes straight ahead and uphill. About 3/4 mile after the last escape ramp the grade eases to 3-4% for about 2 miles and then there is a 6% hill for about 3/4 mile. From this point on the grade is gradual for quite a few miles.

47 and 48 see New Info on page 119.

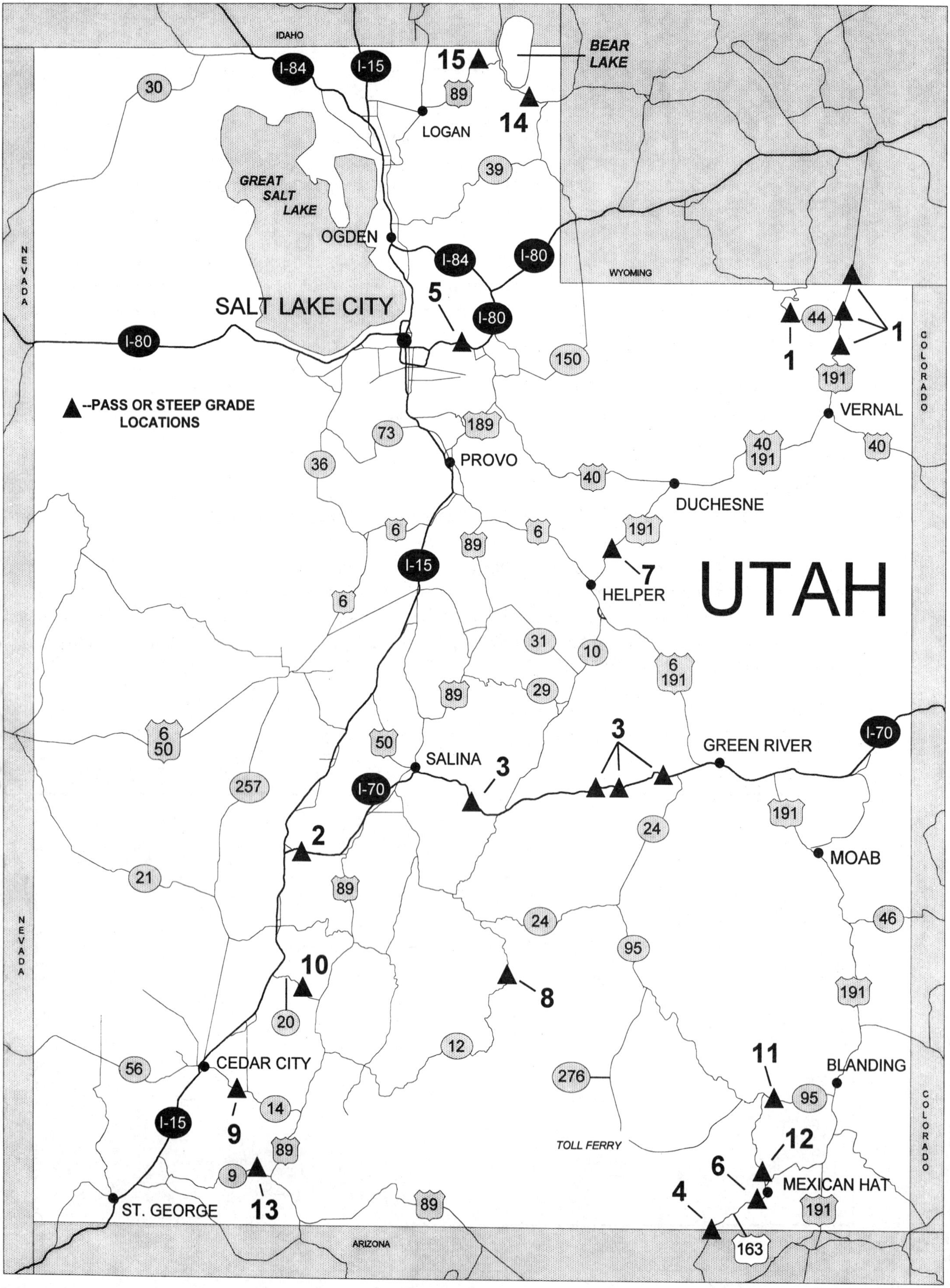
IDAHO
BEAR LAKE
WYOMING
GREAT SALT LAKE
SALT LAKE CITY
OGDEN
LOGAN
NEVADA
COLORADO
ARIZONA
▲--PASS OR STEEP GRADE LOCATIONS
VERNAL
PROVO
DUCHESNE
HELPER
UTAH
SALINA
GREEN RIVER
MOAB
CEDAR CITY
BLANDING
TOLL FERRY
MEXICAN HAT
ST. GEORGE
I-84
I-15
I-80
I-70
30
89
39
44
150
191
73
189
36
40
6
31
10
29
50
257
21
24
46
95
20
12
56
14
9
276
163
1
2
3
4
5
6
7
8
9
10
11
12
13
14
15

UTAH

1. FLAMING GORGE AREA*
2. I-70 AND I-15
3. I-70 SALINA TO GREEN RIVER
4. MONUMENT PASS
5. PARLEY'S SUMMIT
6. US 163 SOUTH OF MEXICAN HAT
7. US 191 HELPER TO DUCHESNE
8. UTAH HIGHWAY 12
9. UTAH HIGHWAY 14
10. UTAH HIGHWAY 20
11. UTAH HIGHWAY 95
12. UTAH HIGHWAY 261
13. ZION NATIONAL PARK (UTAH HIGHWAY 9)

14 and 15 see New Info on page 119

* In both Utah and Wyoming directories.

1 FLAMING GORGE AREA--UTAH AND WYOMING

(Utah Highway 44 between Manila, UT and the junction with US 191)
About 12 miles south of Manila there is a descent for northbounders. Beginning near milepost 16 there is a **5 mile 8% grade** with 30 mph curves. *Use caution on this hill.*

(US 191 Highway between Flaming Gorge Dam and the junction with Utah Highway 44)
Just north of the junction of 191 and 44 there is a sign for northbounders--**"Downgrade next 5 miles."** The 5-6% grade stairsteps down for about 2 miles where there is a brake check area. The next **3 miles are steady 6% downgrade** with 20 mph curves and a bridge at the bottom of the hill.

(US 191 Highway north of Flaming Gorge Dam)
Between Flaming Gorge Dam and the Wyoming state line there are numerous short rolling hills as steep as 6-7%. They are usually 1 mile or less in length. For those coming south on 191 thru Wyoming there is a sign--**"9% grade next 2 1/2 miles."** This sign is near milepost 547 or about 4 miles north of the Utah state line. There are several miles of 3-4% descent before reaching the steep part of the grade. There is a *runaway truck ramp about milepost 548 1/2.* It exits to the right and goes uphill.

(US 191 Highway between the junction with Utah Highway 44 and Vernal, UT)
"Snowtires or chains required Nov. 1 to March 31." About 9 miles south of the 191-44 junction there is a summit (8428'). The northbound descent from the summit continues almost 9 miles back to the junction but it is rolling hills in the 4% range except for the last mile which is about 6% descent.

The southbound descent from the summit begins with about 6 miles of rolling grade, some of which is 5-6%. About milepost 220 1/2 there is a brake check area for southbounders and several warning signs--**"5-8% grades--10 switchbacks next 9 miles"** and "Truck speed limit over 10,000 lbs. 30 mph." There is a good deal of 8% grade included in the descent and the switchbacks are posted at 20 mph. *Use caution on this hill.*

MOUNTAIN TAMER *VARIABLE ENGINE BRAKING* GAS AND DIESEL *SEE AD ON PAGE 3*

UTAH

2   I-70 JUST EAST OF I-15 IN UTAH

There is a summit near milepost 7 on I-70 east of I-15. The descent westbound from the summit starts with about **4 miles of 5-6% grade followed by 1/2 mile of 4%.**

The eastbound descent from the summit begins with rolling 3-5% grade for about 6 miles. **At milepost 13 there is a brake test area and the grade starts down at 4% and soon goes to 5-6%. At milepost 16 1/2 there is a runaway truck ramp.** It exits to the right and is at the same grade as the road. The grade continues past the escape ramp at about 4-5% for 2 miles and then eases to 3-4%.

3   SALINA TO GREEN RIVER, UTAH ON I-70

There are three separate sections of steep grade between Salina and Green River.

About 26 miles east of Salina (near milepost 80 1/2) there is a summit on I-70. The westbound descent is marked--**"Steep grade next 7 miles."** The grade is mostly 3-4% and is somewhat steeper near the bottom. The eastbound descent is marked--**"Steep grade next 8 miles."** The first 3 1/2 miles are about 5% followed by 3 and 4% for about 4 miles.

At milepost 94 there is a sign for eastbound traffic--**"Steep grade"** with no details. During the next 8 or 10 miles there are several short sections of **6% grade** with lesser grade in between as the highway descends into a valley. Westbound traffic will descend into this same valley from about milepost 115. The descent is in stages with 6% grade alternating with lesser grade for about 7 miles.

At milepost 136 there is a brake check area for eastbound traffic and warning signs--**"Trucks over 10,000 lbs. 50 mph speed limit"** and **"6% grade next 6 miles."** The grade is **steady 6%** except for a 1/2 mile section of 4% near the top of the hill. There are *two runaway truck ramps*. **The first is at milepost 139 1/2 and the second is at milepost 141 1/2.** The first escape ramp exits to the right and goes uphill. It is rather short and there is a vertical rock wall that rises from the end of the ramp. So if the gravel bed doesn't stop you, the rock wall gets a chance. The second escape ramp also exits to the right and uphill. **There are 2 miles of 6% grade after the second escape ramp.** There are 45 mph curves during the last 3 miles of the descent.

4   MONUMENT PASS

(on US 163 at Utah-Arizona state line.)
There is very little grade on either side of Monument Pass.

5   PARLEY'S SUMMIT

(on I-80 east of Salt Lake City, UT)

Parley's Summit is at milepost 140 on I-80. This is about 10 miles east of the junction of I-215 and I-80 on the east side of Salt Lake City. The eastbound descent from the summit is about **2 1/2 miles of 4-6% grade.** The westbound descent from the summit has a brake check area and signs warning--**"Check brakes--3-6% grades next 10 miles"** and **"Loaded trucks 40 mph max."** and *"Truck escape ramp--left lane 3 1/2 miles."* **The first 6 miles are steady 6% grade** and *the escape ramp is near the 136 milepost.* It exits to the *left* and goes uphill. There is almost **3 miles of 6% after the escape ramp** followed by 5 miles of 3% grade.

6 US HIGHWAY 163
(south of Mexican Hat, UT)

About milepost 15 there is a sign for northbound traffic--**"6-10% grade next 6 miles"** and there is a brake check area. The grade is not steady for the entire 6 miles but stairsteps down to Mexican Hat with the last 1/2 mile at 10% grade. At the bottom of this 10% hill you cross a bridge and make a hard right into town.

7 US HIGHWAY 191
(between Helper and Duchesne, UT)

This highway may be closed in winter. It is marked--**"Snow tires or chains required Nov. 1 to March 1."** The summit (elev. 9100') is about 29 miles south of Duchesne at milepost 172 1/2. The southbound descent begins with a sign--**"8% grade next 4 1/2 miles." The grade is steady the entire 4 1/2 miles.** The northbound descent is **8% grade for about 2 1/2 miles** where it eases to about **6% for 2 more miles.** The grade then stairsteps down a few miles followed by 3-4% downhill for some distance.

8 UTAH HIGHWAY 12
(between US 89 and Utah Highway 24)

There are many steep grades along this 130 mile stretch of road. Most of these grades are fairly short but can be in the **8 to 12% range**. The longest grades are south of Torrey, UT. About 23 miles south of Torrey there is a summit called Round Top Flat. The northbound descent from the summit is a curvy, stairstepping descent of about **6% for 5 1/2 miles**. Then there is a section of rolling hills for about 4 miles followed by 10 miles of stairstepping grade, some of which is **8%**. The longest single section of 8% grade is about 2 miles long and there are several sections of 1 1/2 miles or less.

The southbound descent from Round Top Flat starts with about 1 1/2 miles of 6% grade and then 1 1/2 miles of rolling uphill grade. After topping out the grade is back downhill at **6-8% for about 5 miles** where it eases to about **4% for several miles**. At this point you are several miles north of Boulder, Utah.

Between Boulder and Escalante there are several sections of steep grade both uphill and down. These can be as steep as **10 or 11%** but they usually don't exceed 2 miles in length. There are more short, steep grades between Escalante and Henrieville including a **one mile stretch marked at 12%.**

Just east of Bryce Canyon there is a **2 mile 8% grade** and just west of Bryce Canyon there is a **2-3 mile stretch of 6%** grade descending into Red Canyon.

UTAH

9 UTAH HIGHWAY 14
(between Cedar City and Long Valley Junction, UT)

Warning signs for this road include--**"8% grades, 25 mph curves, not recommended for semi-trucks, 10,000' summit may be impassable in winter months."** This summit is about 18 miles east of Cedar City. There is a brake check area at the top of the hill.

The westbound descent begins with a sign saying--**"4-8% grades, 25 mph curves next 10 miles."** The grade starts with about **2 miles of 6% and then goes to 8% for 3 1/2 miles and then 6% for 5 miles. Then 4 miles of 4% which adds up to 14 1/2 miles of grade** with 25 and 35 mph curves.

The eastbound descent from the summit is spread over a longer distance but still has some **6-8% sections of grade. One section is about 3 1/2 miles long and another is about 4 miles long.** Most of the rest is 2-5% grade. It is about 23 1/2 miles from the summit to the junction with US 89.

10 SUMMIT ON UTAH HIGHWAY 20
(between I-15 and US 89)

This summit is at milepost 10 (10 miles east of I-15) and the grade is posted at **8% going both directions from the summit.** The westbound descent seemed to be somewhat less than 8% but the steep part of the descent eases about 2 1/4 miles down from the summit. The grade is about 4% the next 2 miles followed by about 3 miles of 5-6%. The road is 2 lane with 45 mph curves. The descent totals about **7 miles of 4 to 8% grade**.

The eastbound descent starts down about 8% and gradually lessens over the next 3 1/2 miles until it nearly flattens out. The road is 2 lane with 35 mph curves.

11 UTAH HIGHWAY 95
(between Blanding, UT and the junction of 95 and 261 highways)

About 4 miles east of 261 and 95 highway there is a descent for eastbound traffic. Near milepost 97 there is a sign--**"5-9% grade."** The descent is about 10 miles long but is not steady. There are **5-6% grades for 8 miles and 8% grades the last 2 miles.** There are more 8% grades both up and downhill from this point to Blanding but they are 2 miles or less in length.

12 UTAH HIGHWAY 261
(north of Mexican Hat, UT)

At milepost 10 on highway 261 there are warning signs for southbound traffic--**"5-10% grades next 3 miles."** and **"20 mph curves next 3 miles."** About milepost 9 1/2 the **road turns to gravel** and becomes very narrow with extremely sharp hairpin turns. It is about a 1000' drop over the side. The road is less than 2 lanes wide in places. After 2 1/2 miles of gravel the road is paved again but remains narrow and steep for another 1/2 mile. The grade then goes to about 4% for 1/2 mile and then eases to the valley floor.

UTAH

13 ZION NATIONAL PARK
(Utah Highway 9)

Commercial trucking is prohibited thru Zion National Park.

There is a summit on Utah Highway 9 about 7 miles east of the entrance to the park. The eastbound descent to the junction with US 89 is mostly 2-3% grade with 3 short sections of 6% grade.

The westbound descent is about **15 miles in length**. The 7 miles to the park entrance are variable grade--some rolling up and down, some stairstepping down and **some steady 4-5% downhill**. The grade continues past the park entrance until the tunnel is reached.

The tunnel was built in 1930 and is 1.1 miles long. The tunnel is restricted or prohibited to some vehicles. If the vehicle is over 7' 10" wide including mirrors or over 11' 4" in height it must be escorted thru the tunnel. Rangers are stationed at each end of the tunnel 8:00 AM to 8:00 PM daily March thru October. Oversized vehicles are prohibited from passing thru the tunnel any other time of day. Winter escorts are arranged at entrance stations, visitor center or by calling 772-3256. Vehicles over 13' 1" high are prohibited. There are other weight and length restrictions. Call for details.

The downgrade thru the tunnel is about 5% and the speed limit is 15 mph. After leaving the tunnel there are about 3 miles of 5-6% grade with 15 and 20 mph curves.

14 and 15 see New Info on page 119

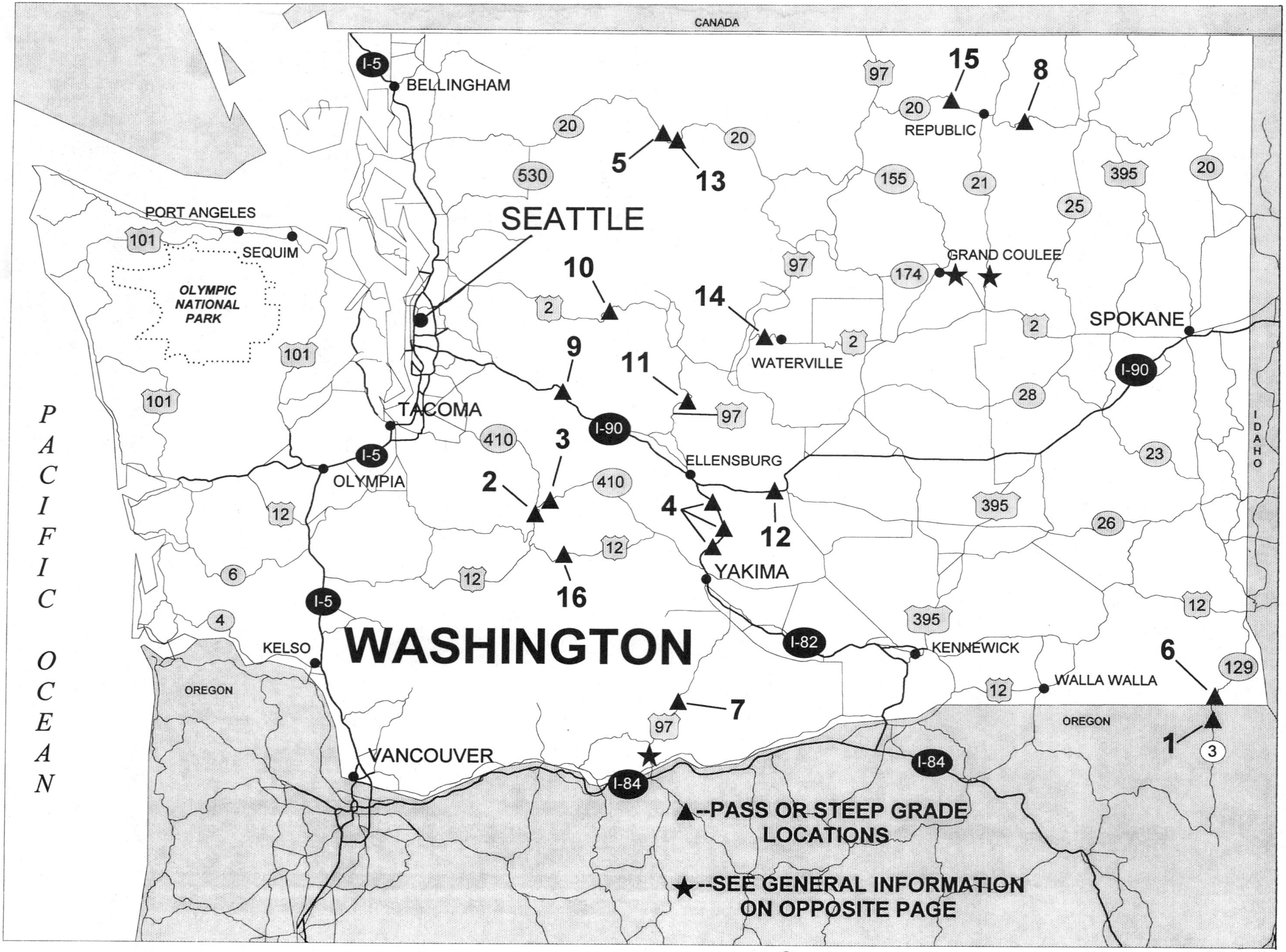
CANADA
BELLINGHAM
PORT ANGELES
SEQUIM
OLYMPIC NATIONAL PARK
SEATTLE
TACOMA
OLYMPIA
KELSO
VANCOUVER
WASHINGTON
ELLENSBURG
YAKIMA
WATERVILLE
GRAND COULEE
REPUBLIC
SPOKANE
KENNEWICK
WALLA WALLA
OREGON
IDAHO
PACIFIC OCEAN
▲--PASS OR STEEP GRADE LOCATIONS
★--SEE GENERAL INFORMATION ON OPPOSITE PAGE

WASHINGTON

1. BUFORD GRADE*
2. CAYUSE PASS
3. CHINOOK PASS
4. I-82 YAKIMA TO ELLENSBURG
5. RAINY PASS
   (see WASHINGTON PASS)
6. RATTLESNAKE GRADE*
   (see BUFORD GRADE)
7. SATUS PASS
8. SHERMAN PASS
9. SNOQUALMIE PASS
10. STEVENS PASS
11. SWAUK PASS
12. VANTAGE HILL
13. WASHINGTON PASS
14. WATERVILLE--ORONDO HILL
15. WAUCONDA SUMMIT
16. WHITE PASS

* In both Washington and Oregon directories.

General information for the state of Washington:

When a road approaches a river crossing in the state of Washington there is a good possibility of steep descents--some may be long, some short.

Examples:

★ Where Washington State highway 21 northbound approaches the Columbia River at Keller Ferry there are about **5 miles of 6% descent** with numerous hairpin turns. On the other side of the river the descent is spread over a long distance and there are just some rolling hills as you get near the river.

★ There is a **3 mile 6% descent** on Washington State highway 174 westbound as you approach Grand Coulee Dam.

★ As US 97 southbound approaches the Columbia River from Goldendale, Washington there is a descent of about **6 miles at 5%** grade. There is a stop sign and an intersection about 4 1/2 miles down from the top.

Other examples: see Waterville-Orondo Hill and Vantage Hill in the Washington section of this book. (See the above index.)

Eric's RV PERFORMANCE CENTER *Established 1972*

1-800-488-3697

ARE DOWNHILL MOUNTAIN PASSES A THREAT TO YOU, OR DO YOU LACK ENOUGH POWER TO CLIMB THAT STEEP PASS? CALL THE PROFESSIONALS AT ERIC'S RV PERFORMANCE CENTER FOR EXPERT EXHAUST BRAKE ADVICE OR BANKS POWERPACK AND TURBO PRODUCTS.

Engine Exhaust Braking: Give your RV and your mind a break. Engine exhaust brakes reduce dangerous brake fade and expensive repairs, as well as preventing serious engine damage. We have **BD** and **Pac** brakes for diesel engines.

Gear Splitters: Enjoy optimum towing power with correct gearing and engine RPM, better mileage and longer engine life with an array of choices for the best gear combinations from **Gear Vendors, US Gear,** and **Mitchell Splitters**.

Eric's RV Performance Center
275 S. 7th Avenue
Sequim, WA 98382

WASHINGTON

1 BUFORD GRADE
(on Oregon Highway 3 north of Enterprise, OR)
RATTLESNAKE GRADE
(on Washington Highway 129 south of Clarkston, WA)

The Grande Ronde River flows near the Washington-Oregon border on the eastern edge of these states. Washington State Highway 129 crosses the river and a few miles later crosses the state line where it becomes Oregon State Highway 3.

There are long, steep descents to the river from both north and south. The descent on the Washington side is called Rattlesnake Grade. The descent on the Oregon side is called Buford Grade.

The descent from the north down Rattlesnake Grade begins about milepost 14 1/2. There is **no steep grade warning.** There is a sign stating--**"25 mph curves next 9 miles."** The first mile is about 3-4% grade. The next **9 miles are about 6%** with constant 20, 25, and 30 mph curves all the way down.

The descent from the south down Buford Grade also begins with about 1 mile of 3-4% grade and then about **9 1/2 miles of 6%** and then 1/2 mile of 3-4% before reaching the river. There are 20, 25, and 30 mph curves all the way to the bottom. The Oregon-Washington state line is crossed about 6 miles down the hill. **Use caution on these descents.**

It is customary for logging trucks and other local truckers to use the CB radio to announce their position on these grades. They call out which milepost they're passing, which hill they're on, whether they are going up or down, and if they are loaded or empty. The road is very narrow and winding so you usually can't see very far ahead. Some of the curves are too tight for two trucks to get by each other so the announcement of position helps avoid problems.

2 CAYUSE PASS elev. 4675'
(on Washington Highway 123 in Mt. Rainier National Park, WA)

Commercial vehicles are not allowed in the park. This road is closed in winter. The summit of Cayuse Pass is at the junction of Washington State highways 410 and 123.

State highway 123 is a narrow, winding 2 lane road. From the summit the descent is a **steady 6% for about 8 miles** with 25 and 35 mph curves. **The next 8 miles are 3-5% grade** but with flat stretches alternating with downgrade.

3 CHINOOK PASS elev. 5430'
(on Washington Highway 410 in the eastern side of Mt. Rainier National Park, WA)

Commercial vehicles are not allowed in the park. This road is closed in winter.

Going west on State 410 (which is actually almost due north) the descent from the summit of Chinook Pass begins with about 1/2 mile of 6% grade. Over the next 3/4 mile the grade gradually eases to 2-3% but then it's downhill at **5-6% for the next 8 1/2 miles.** It is a narrow, winding, rough 2 lane road with 25 and 35 mph curves.

The eastbound descent starts with 5-6% downhill grade and 35 mph curves. After about 1 1/2 miles the road opens up some but the grade remains about 6%. The road is wider and smoother than on the other side of the pass. The grade is a **steady 5-6% for about 6 miles** down from the summit. At this point the grade eases to 4% and then 3% and about 9 miles down from the summit the descent becomes rolling hills.

WASHINGTON

4 INTERSTATE 82
(between Yakima and Ellensburg, WA)

There are three ridges on I-82 between Yakima and Ellensburg.

The northbound descent from Manastash Ridge toward Ellensburg is about **5 miles of 5-6% grade**. Manastash Ridge is about milepost 8.

The southbound descent from South Umptanum Ridge toward Yakima is about **4 miles of 4-6% grade.** South Umptanum Ridge is about milepost 21.

The up and down grades between these two ridges are either 5-6% for a couple of miles or 2-4% for longer distances.

5 RAINY PASS--see WASHINGTON PASS

6 RATTLESNAKE GRADE--see BUFORD GRADE

7 SATUS PASS elev. 3107'
(on US 97 north of Goldendale, WA)

The summit of Satus Pass is at milepost 27 on US 97 north of Goldendale and south of Toppenish, Washington. There is a good deal of truck traffic on US 97.

The southbound descent from the summit of Satus Pass begins with about 2 1/2 miles of 3-5% grade. Then it's uphill and down a couple of times to about milepost 20. Then 5-6% downhill for about a mile before the grade eases and it's 2-4% for the next 3 miles.

The descent on the north side of Satus Pass has a warning sign--**"Steep grade--5% next 4 miles."** The first 4 miles are about 5% as promised and then there are about **2 1/2 miles of 4% grade**.

8 SHERMAN PASS elev. 5575'
(on Washington Highway 20 east of Republic, WA)

The summit of Sherman Pass is about 15 miles east of Republic. **Vehicles over 10,000 lbs. must use chains when required.**

The eastbound descent from the summit begins with about **1 mile of 5% grade and then 3 miles of 5-6% grade.** The grade then begins to ease to **4-5% for 2 miles** and then to 3% for 6 miles with 2 or 3 short 5% hills thrown in. The **total descent is about 12 miles** with the first 4 miles the steepest.

The westbound descent begins with a sign saying--"6% grade next 10 miles--trucks use lower gear." The sign does not lie but does not tell all. After the promised 10 miles of 6%, the grade eases to about 3% for 3 miles. Then up a short hill and down again for 1 1/2 miles at 6% thru the junction of 21 and 20 highways. Both sides of this pass have 30-45 mph curves. **Use caution on this hill.**

GV GEAR VENDORS UNDER/OVERDRIVE™ MORE POWER... BETTER ECONOMY. See ad on Page 29

103

WASHINGTON

9 SNOQUALMIE PASS elev. 3022'
(on I-90 east of North Bend, WA)
Chain up areas are provided for vehicles over 10,000 lbs.

There is very little descent on the east side of Snoqualmie Pass. There is about 2 1/2 miles of 3% and then the grade is even flatter for 8 or 9 miles. After that are some rolling hills--some of them about 4%--both uphill and down.

The westbound descent from the summit of Snoqualmie begins with a sign--**"Steep grade next 4.5 miles--trucks use lower gear."** The **first 4 miles are 6%** followed by 3/4 mile of 4-5%, and 2 miles of 3-4%, and 2 miles of 2-3%.

10 STEVENS PASS elev. 4061'
(on US 2 east of Skykomish, WA)

The westbound descent of Stevens Pass is about **6 1/2 miles of 5-6% grade** with 40 mph curves. The first 4 1/2 miles down from the summit are 4 lane. It then turns to 3 lane and then 2 lane.

The eastbound descent is **3-4 miles of 5-6% grade**. The road changes from 4 lane to 2 lane six miles down from the summit.

11 SWAUK PASS elev. 4102' also known as BLEWETT PASS
(on US 97 south of Dryden, WA)

The maps show Swauk Pass on US 97 and Blewett Pass on the old road, but the summit on US 97 is marked Blewett Pass with Swauk Pass's elevation. In any case, the pass on US 97 has a **3 mile 3-5% descent** on the north side. The south side is **2 miles of 6% descent followed by 3 or 4 miles of 3-5% grade.**

12 VANTAGE HILL
(on I-90 east of Ellensburg, WA at the Columbia River)

This is one of many places in the state of Washington where the approach to a river includes a long or steep descent. The eastbound descent begins about milepost 126 on I-90 and continues to the Columbia River almost **11 miles** down the hill. **The top half of this hill is 3-4% grade and the bottom half is about 5%.** There are about 2 miles of 5% grade on the east side of the river.

13 WASHINGTON PASS elev. 5477'
(on Washington Highway 20 west of Winthrop, WA)
RAINY PASS elev. 4855'
(just west of Washington Pass)

Washington State Highway 20 is **closed during most of the winter** between Mazama and Ross Dam. It is a good 2 lane road with passing lanes during the climbs.

The eastbound descent from the summit of Washington Pass begins with a sign saying--**"7% grade next 7 miles."** There are 30 and 40 mph curves during the descent and the grade seems to ease a bit before the 7 miles are covered. **Use caution on this hill.**

The westbound descent is about **4 miles of 6-7% grade.** At this point the climb to the summit of Rainy Pass begins. The summit is reached after a 1 1/2 mile 5-6% climb.

The sign for westbound traffic at the summit of Rainy Pass says--**"6% grade next 4 miles."** After descending the 4 miles the grade does flatten out for about 3 miles but there is more descent to come. After the 3 mile flat section there is a **3 mile 3-5% downhill grade** followed by a 1 mile flat section and then a sign--**"Steep grade next 3 miles." This grade is 5-6%.** There is a lot of downhill left until Newhalem is reached 26 miles from this sign. The descent is broken up by rolling hills or flat spots but there are several stretches where the 5-6% downgrades last for 2 or 3 miles. There are many 20-35 mph curves during the descent. There are **two tunnels** in the last 3 miles before reaching Newhalem.

14 WATERVILLE--ORONDO HILL
(on US 2 between Waterville and Orondo, WA)

This is one of many places in the state of Washington where the approach to a river includes a long or steep descent. A little over a mile west of Waterville is a sign saying--**"All trucks must stop--check brakes--1 mile ahead."** At the brake check turnout is another sign--**"6% grade next 6 miles--trucks use lower gear." The grade is steady and is closer to 7 miles long.** US 2 is a good 2 lane highway with 35 and 40 mph curves all the way down the hill. *There are no escape ramps.*

Six miles down from the top of the hill is another sign--**"Stop sign 1 mile"** and the grade continues down. About 1/2 mile later US 2 splits to the left and US 97 splits to the right. *The stop sign warning applies to both roads and you must have some brakes left because if you can't make the stop sign the alternatives are not very good.* **Use caution on this hill.**

15 WAUCONDA SUMMIT elev. 4310'
(on Washington Highway 20 west of Republic, WA)

Wauconda Summit is only 3 miles east of Wauconda, Washington. Both sides of this hill are pretty tame with descents that have very short sections of 5-6% grade. Most of the grade is in the 3-4% range and the descent on both sides is only 3-4 miles.

SCRATCH HERE

IF YOU *DON'T* SMELL BURNING BRAKES YOU MUST OWN A

OUNTAIN TAMER
VARIABLE ENGINE BRAKING
GAS$_{A^N_D}$DIESEL
Also High Performance Torque Converters

DECEL-O-MATIC CORP
SEE AD ON PAGE 3

WASHINGTON

16 WHITE PASS elev. 4500'
(on US 12 west of Yakima, WA)

The summit of White Pass is about milepost 151 on US 12. The eastbound descent from the summit begins with about 2 1/2 miles of 2-3% grade. Then there is a warning sign--**"Steep grade next 7 miles."** Most of this 7 miles is **4-5% grade** with 30 mph curves.

The westbound descent from the summit starts with a warning sign--**"6% grade next 4 miles."** The hill descends in a stairstep fashion for a while with places where the grade eases for a little while. Four miles down from the summit is another warning sign--**"6% grade next 2 miles."** It is a winding 2 lane road. After this 2 mile section the grade eases for almost a mile and then there is another sign--**"6% grade next 6 miles."** There is a *runaway truck ramp 2 1/2 miles down from this sign* (or about 10 miles down from the summit). *The escape ramp goes off to the right at an angle that could be a problem for a fast moving truck.* The **6% grade continues for 3 miles past the escape ramp** and then there are rolling hills for 1 1/2 miles followed by another mile of 6% downhill and then more rolling hills.

WASHINGTON

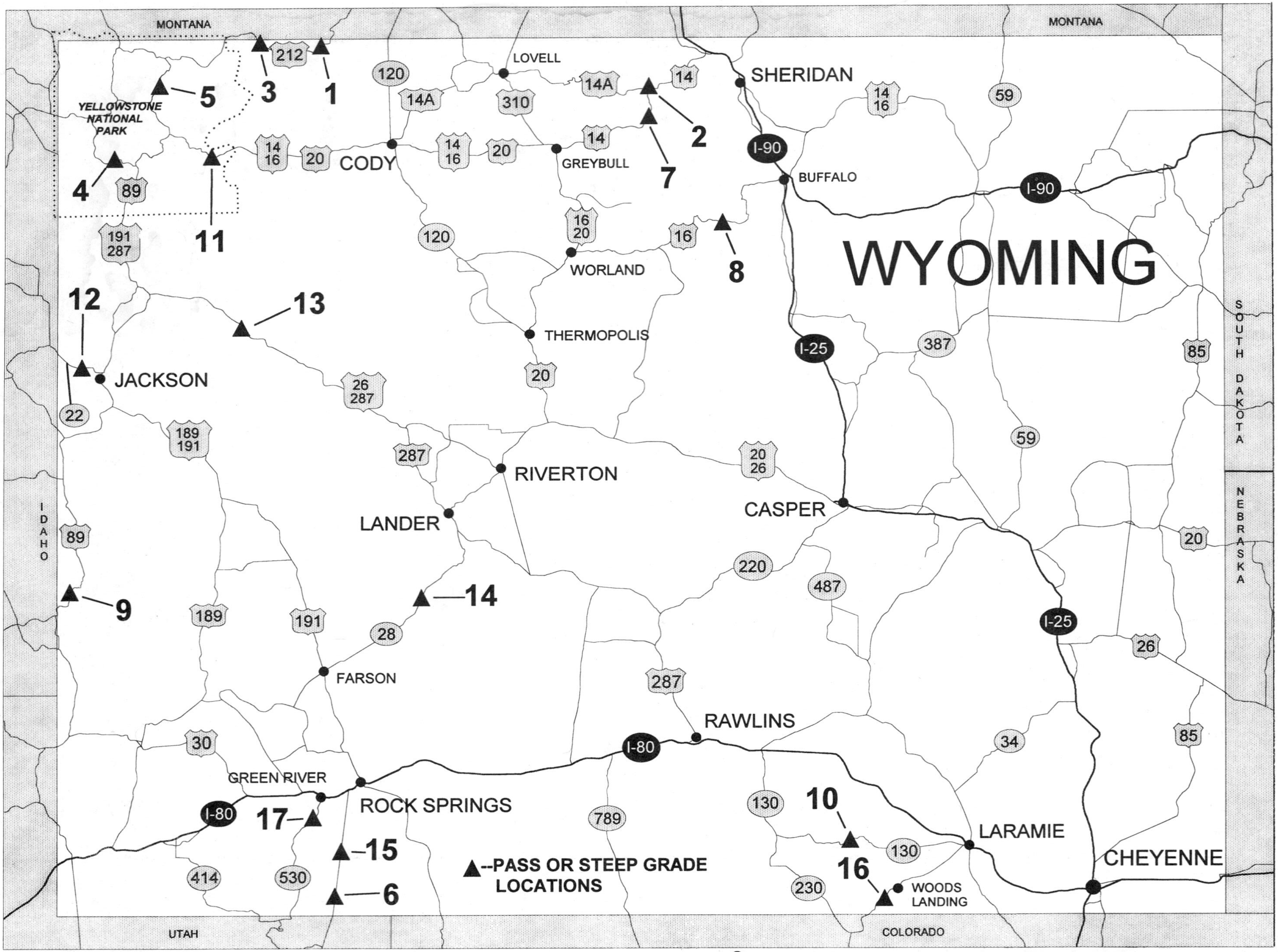
WYOMING
MONTANA
MONTANA
SOUTH DAKOTA
NEBRASKA
IDAHO
UTAH
COLORADO
YELLOWSTONE NATIONAL PARK
SHERIDAN
BUFFALO
LOVELL
CODY
GREYBULL
WORLAND
THERMOPOLIS
JACKSON
RIVERTON
LANDER
CASPER
FARSON
RAWLINS
GREEN RIVER
ROCK SPRINGS
LARAMIE
CHEYENNE
WOODS LANDING
I-90
I-25
I-80
▲--PASS OR STEEP GRADE LOCATIONS

WYOMING

1. BEAR TOOTH PASS *
2. BURGESS JUNCTION
3. COLTER PASS*
   (see BEAR TOOTH PASS)
4. CRAIG PASS
5. DUNRAVEN PASS
6. FLAMING GORGE AREA **
7. GRANITE PASS
   (see BURGESS JUNCTION)

8. POWDER RIVER PASS
9. SALT RIVER PASS
10. SNOWY RANGE PASS
11. SYLVAN PASS
12. TETON PASS
13. TOGOWOTEE PASS

14 thru 17 see New Info on page 119

*In both Montana and Wyoming directories.
**In both Utah and Wyoming directories.

1 BEAR TOOTH PASS elev. 10947' and COLTER PASS elev. 8000'
(on US 212 west of Red Lodge, MT)

Bear Tooth Pass is aptly named. It is a bear of a pass. **Use caution on this pass.** The Montana-Wyoming state line is near the summit. The Montana side of the pass is the most difficult with a very narrow, rough, winding, and steep descent. **The pass is usually closed to winter travel** and the weather can change rapidly in any season. Bear Tooth Pass has an east summit and a west summit. The descent from the west summit to the bottom on the Montana side (in other words-eastbound) is **22 miles of 6-8% grade**. The road is narrow and there are few places one can pull over alongside the road if need be. There are numerous 15, 20, 25 mph hairpin turns, many of these unmarked.

Descending eastbound from the west summit of Bear Tooth the first 1 1/2 miles are about 8% downhill grade followed by 1 1/2 miles of 5-7% grade uphill to the east summit.

The first **4 miles** downhill from the east summit are **about 8%** with 20 mph hairpins and other curves. At the end of the 4 miles there is a sign stating--**"Winding road next 15 miles."** The worst of it only lasts about **10 miles.** This is **steady 5-6% grade**, almost continuous 15 to 25 mph curves, and narrow road with very little shoulder. After this 10 mile section the road opens up a little with speed limits increased to about 50 mph but the grade is still in the **5-6% range for another 3-4 miles.** *Brakes may be hot by this time--use caution about increasing speed.* The grade will begin to ease after the 3-4 miles of 50 mph speed limits and the descent will be completed about 7 miles west of Red Lodge, Montana.

The westbound descent from the west summit of Bear Tooth is about **6-7% grade** but it is not as steady as the Montana side. There are some places where the grade eases or nearly flattens for short stretches--maybe as little as 1/4 mile--and then goes back down. There are many 15, 20, 25 mph hairpin turns and curves--some unmarked--and the road does not improve until about 13 miles down from the summit where it gets wider and smoother. About 18 1/2 miles down from the summit is a sharp curve with a bridge in the middle of it. If you are from a cold climate you already know that bridges can be icy when the rest of the road is not. This bridge could be a problem in bad weather.

Some of the steeper sections of this descent are farther down the mountain. The total trip down is about 21 miles and the last few miles have some grade in the 7-8% range.

If you continue westbound you will go over **Colter Pass** but after Bear Tooth you probably won't even notice it. Colter Pass summit is about 1 1/2 miles east of Cooke City and about 5 miles east of Yellowstone Park's entrance. The road is rolling throughout this area and there are no long climbs or descents on either side of Colter Pass.

WYOMING

2 BURGESS JUNCTION and the "OH, MY GOD HILL"
(on US 14ALT. west of Ranchester, WY)
GRANITE PASS elev. 9033' and SHELL CANYON
(on US 14 west of Ranchester, WY)

Ranchester, Wyoming is about 14 miles north of Sheridan, Wyoming. If traveling west on US 14 you will climb to Burgess Junction where US 14 and US 14 Alt. divide. US 14 goes over Granite Pass and down Shell Canyon to Greybull, Wyoming. US 14 Alt. goes over Bald Mountain and down what the locals call the "Oh, My God Hill" into Lovell, Wyoming.

The descent on US 14 thru Shell Canyon is 5-7% for 18 miles. The descent on US 14 Alt. is posted at 10% for 10 miles down the "OMG Hill" but there is an additional 4 miles of 8% grade after the 10 miles of 10%. This is a very difficult hill in either direction for large or heavy vehicles.

There is a good deal of open range in this area and there is often livestock on the roads.

First, we'll start with the descent from Burgess Jct. to the east down towards Ranchester. The first 11 miles from the junction going east will be up and down with 5-6% grades and 30 and 40 mph curves. The next 2 1/2 miles are downhill with the grade changing from 6% to 2 or 3% and then back to 6%. At this point, which is 13 miles east of the junction, there is a truck warning sign--**"Steep grade next 9 miles."** And indeed there is. **Over the next 9 miles the grade is 5-7%** with many 25 and 30 mph curves. It is a good 2 lane road with some stretches of 3 lane. From here the grade eases over the next couple of miles.

To begin the westbound descent we'll stay on US 14 west from Burgess Jct. and then we'll come back and describe the descent on US 14 Alt.

From Burgess Jct. west on US 14 the speed limit is 55 and the grade rolls up and down for about 10 miles to the summit of Granite Pass. From the summit the first mile starts steep and then eases some and then a truck warning sign says--**"Steep grade next 18 miles." From this point the grade is about 5-7% for almost the entire descent.** There are many 35 to 55 mph curves in the upper part of the descent. There is a section of higher speed limit before entering the sharper curves of the canyon. The speed limit is 55 and the grade is still steep. *This combination of grade and speed can very quickly lead to over heated brakes. Use caution because there is still a long descent ahead.*

There is a truck warning sign 11 1/2 miles down from the summit--**"Steep grade next 7 miles."** There are constant 20, 25, 30, and 35 mph curves and **the grade remains in the 5 to 7% range.** *Needless to say, this is a very long and steep hill for heavy vehicles. Equipment and drivers need to be in good condition.*

The descent from Burgess Jct. on US 14 Alt. begins with a sign at the junction--**"All trucks, RV's and vehicles with trailers must stop and read sign at turnout ahead."** The sign is a map of the routes that US 14 and US 14 Alt. take as they divide and descend from the junction. This information is included on the map:

US 14 westbound to Shell Canyon, 5-7% grade--sharp curves--4600' drop in elevation in 18 miles. This is an *average* of about 5% for the entire 18 miles.

US 14 Alt. westbound has turnouts for trucks and RV's to check brakes, *3 runaway truck ramps,* **turnouts to cool brakes--10% downgrade for 10 miles--sharp curves--3600' drop in elevation in 10 miles.** (The sign doesn't mention the 4 miles of 8% grade after the 10 miles of 10%.)

The first 20 miles west of the junction on US 14 Alt. is rolling hills and then there is a warning sign--**"Brake check turnout--All trucks, RV's, vehicles with trailers must stop 1 mile"** and

(continued)

(BURGESS JUNCTION continued)

"10% grade next 10 miles--sharp curves--check brakes." (Don't forget the 4 miles of 8% grade they didn't mention that comes after the 10 miles of 10%.) **The first runaway truck ramp is about 2 1/2 miles down the hill from this sign.** It exits to the right and goes downhill and then uphill. The signs say--"**All vehicles use lower gear.**" Two and one half miles down from the first runaway truck ramp there is a brake cooling turnout. **The next runaway truck ramp is almost 2 miles past the cooling turnout or 4 1/4 miles after the first escape ramp.** It is an upsloping ramp. **The third runaway truck ramp is 1 1/4 miles after the second ramp.** It is a downhill ramp. **There is 6 miles of steep grade left after the last escape ramp. There are 2 miles of 10% and 4 miles of 8% grade left to the bottom of the hill.** *This is a very dangerous hill for heavy vehicles.*

3   COLTER PASS--see BEAR TOOTH PASS

4   CRAIG PASS elev. 8261'
(on Grand Loop Road between West Thumb Junction and Old Faithful in Yellowstone Park, WY)

Craig Pass is on a section of the Grand Loop Road that is in good repair as of Fall, 1993. The road crosses the Continental Divide twice. The first time is about 4 miles west of West Thumb. The elevation is about 650' higher than West Thumb. The second crossing of the Divide is about 6 miles farther west. This crossing is about 520' higher than West Thumb. The entire stretch of road between Old Faithful and West Thumb is rolling hills. There are some 5-6% sections but they are short. The speed limit is 45 mph but there are some slower curves.

5   DUNRAVEN PASS elev. 8859'
(on Grand Loop Road south of Tower Junction in Yellowstone National Park, WY)

Dunraven Pass is south of Tower Junction on the Grand Loop Road in Yellowstone Park. Most of this section of the Grand Loop Road is narrow, rough and winding.

From the summit, near Mt. Washburn, the descent northbound starts with about 1 1/2 miles of rolling hills. The **next 9 miles are a fairly steady descent in the 6% range** with many curves and some hairpin turns. It is a rough 2 lane road. During the last 2 1/2 miles into Tower Junction there are some steep upgrades and sharp curves.

The southbound descent from the summit of Dunraven Pass begins with **3 miles of 5-6% downgrade.** Then the road surface improves and there are rolling hills into Canyon Village Junction.

6 FLAMING GORGE AREA--UTAH AND WYOMING

(Utah Highway 44 between Manila, UT and the junction with US 191)
About 12 miles south of Manila there is a descent for northbounders. Beginning near milepost 16 there is a **5 mile 8% grade** with 30 mph curves. **Use caution on this hill.**

(US 191 Highway between Flaming Gorge Dam and the junction with Utah Highway 44)
Just north of the junction of 191 and 44 there is a sign for northbounders--**"Downgrade next 5 miles."** The 5-6% grade stairsteps down for about 2 miles where there is a brake check area. The next **3 miles are steady 6% downgrade** with 20 mph curves and a bridge at the bottom of the hill.

(US 191 Highway north of Flaming Gorge Dam)
Between Flaming Gorge Dam and the Wyoming state line there are numerous short rolling hills as steep as 6-7%. They are usually 1 mile or less in length. For those coming south on 191 thru Wyoming there is a sign--**"9% grade next 2 1/2 miles."** This sign is near milepost 547 or about 4 miles north of the Utah state line. There are several miles of 3-4% descent before reaching the steep part of the grade. There is a **runaway truck ramp about milepost 548 1/2.** It exits to the right and goes uphill.

(US 191 Highway between the junction with Utah Highway 44 and Vernal, UT)
"Snowtires or chains required Nov. 1 to March 31." About 9 miles south of the 191-44 junction there is a summit (8428'). The northbound descent from the summit continues almost 9 miles back to the junction but it is rolling hills in the 4% range except for the last mile which is about 6% descent.

The southbound descent from the summit begins with about 6 miles of rolling grade, some of which is 5-6%. About milepost 220 1/2 there is a brake check area for southbounders and several warning signs--**"5-8% grades--10 switchbacks next 9 miles"** and **"Truck speed limit over 10,000 lbs. 30 mph."** There is a good deal of 8% grade included in the descent and the switchbacks are posted at 20 mph. Use caution on this hill.

7 GRANITE PASS--see BURGESS JUNCTION

8 POWDER RIVER PASS elev. 9666'
(on US 16 between Worland and Buffalo, WY)

Ten Sleep Canyon lies west of Powder River Pass and a westbound descent of Powder River Pass must include the descent thru the canyon. Much of this area is open range and there are often cattle on the highway.

The westbound descent from the summit begins with a truck warning sign--**"Steep grade next 1 mile."** The speed limit is 50 and it is a good 2 lane road. After 1 mile downhill there are some short rolling hills in the 6% range and then back downhill. About 2 3/4 miles down from the summit is a sign--**"Steep grade next 18 miles." The grade varies from 5-7% for the next 5 miles** before rolling up and down for a mile or so. There are 35 mph curves.

About 9 miles down from the summit there is a sign reading--**"Brake check turnout"** and the downhill grade is about 6%. During the next mile the grade eases somewhat and then a sign--**"6% grade next 10 miles."** One quarter mile down there is a sign--*"Runaway truck ramp 4 miles."* These grade and escape ramp warnings are repeated every 2 miles. The grade is pretty constant with 40 mph curves.

The runaway truck ramp is 16 miles down from the summit of Powder River Pass. There are **4 miles of steep grade after the escape ramp** with 40 mph curves and 25 mph hairpin turns and then a couple of miles of lesser grade before leaving the canyon. **Use caution on this hill.**

The eastbound descent from the summit begins with a truck warning sign--**"Steep grade next 4 miles--trucks use lower gear."** The **first 2 1/2 miles are 6-7%** with 45 and 50 mph curves. The grade eases a bit for about 1 1/2 miles and then it becomes an up and down ride for the next 20 miles.

At this point there is another truck warning sign--**"Steep grade--7% next 5 miles--truck turnout 1500'--check brakes."** *There are two runaway truck ramps.* There are warning signs about every 1/2 mile as you approach the **first escape ramp.** It **exits to the** *LEFT.* *You must cross the oncoming lane of traffic to use the escape ramp.* It is an upsloping ramp.

The **7% grade continues** and *there is another runaway truck ramp 1 1/2 miles after the first one.* This one is on the right side of the road and goes down over a little rise and then is about parallel with the road. The grade eases about this time and a mile later the descent is pretty much over.

9 SALT RIVER PASS elev. 7610'
(on US 89 south of Afton and Smoot, WY)

Salt River Pass is about the same on the north slope as it is on the south slope. It is a good 2 lane road with 50 mph speed limit. At the summit there is a brake check turnout on both sides of the road. The south slope is **fairly steady 7% grade for about 3 1/2 miles** with ample warning signs. The north slope is **7% for 3 miles** with warning signs.

WYOMING

10 SNOWY RANGE PASS elev. 10847'
(on Wyoming Highway 130 west of Laramie, WY)

Snowy Range Pass is closed to vehicles over 36,000 lbs. gross weight. It is often closed to all traffic in winter. It is a good 2 lane road. **Use caution on this pass.**

Starting from the summit (12 miles west of Centennial, Wyoming) the eastbound descent begins with rolling hills for about 2 1/2 miles. At this point there is a sign--**"Steep grade next 10 miles."** The **grade starts out around 4% and then 5% and then about 2 miles of 6% grade** with 40 mph curves and a couple of 20 mph hairpin turns. Soon there is a sign saying--**"7% grade next 4 miles"** and during the next 4 miles there are numerous curves at about 40 mph. At the end of this 4 mile stretch we are about 10 miles down from the summit and only 2 miles from Centennial. These 2 miles are up and down with 35 and 45 mph curves and fairly steep grades that continue right into Centennial.

The westbound descent from the summit of Snowy Range Pass begins with a 20 mph hairpin turn and 5-6% grade. The grade changes several times during the next 4 1/2 miles. It is in the 3-6% range. Four miles down from the summit is a sign saying--**"Steep grade next 10 miles." The first 4 miles are 5-6%** with 40 mph curves. At this point there is another sign--**"5% grade next 6 miles." It is closer to 7 miles and the grade is constant 5%.** The speed limit is 55 mph but the road is still curvy.

Fifteen miles down from the summit the descent is concluded. About 2 1/2 miles later the road narrows considerably with no shoulder and a rough surface and remains that way for about 9 miles. One mile before the junction with State highway 230 it improves.

11 SYLVAN PASS elev. 8559'
(between Fishing Bridge and the east entrance of Yellowstone National Park, WY)

The summit of Sylvan Pass is about 18 miles east of Fishing Bridge Village. The summit is 8559' in elevation and Fishing Bridge is about 7740' so the descent westbound from the summit is only about an 800' drop in elevation spread over about 12 miles. There are some 5-6% grades and many sharp curves but most of the descent is rolling hills. The last few miles are along the edge of Yellowstone Lake.

The eastbound descent towards the east entrance of the park is about a 1500' drop in elevation in 6 miles. It is a **steady 6-7% descent for about 4 1/2 miles**. The last 1 1/2 miles before reaching the park entrance are about 5-6% grade with rolling hills. There are 25 & 35 mph curves during the descent.

Improve Horsepower & Fuel Mileage

~GMC, P-30, Dodge Class A 440, and Ford Chassis motorhome complete header & muffler systems.
~3" muffler kits for most tow vehicles.
  18% H.P. and 9% mileage gain.
~Headers and muffler kits for most tow vehicles.
  30-55 H.P. increase and up to 2 M.P.G. We use Doug Thorley Try Y Lifetime guaranteed headers.
~All systems smog legal. Utilize stock catalytic converter.
~All systems made of 14 guage aluminized tubing.
~Systems tuned for pulling power at lower RPM and part throttle.
~K&N air filters, IPD sway bars, & computer chips also available.

JARDINE PERFORMANCE EXHAUST
P.O. Box 9222, Jackson Hole, WY 83002
1-800-934-3569

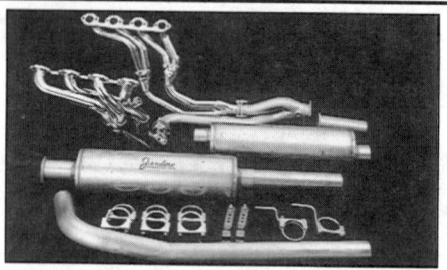

Pictured above: system for 1993 1/2 thru 1996 Ford 460 F-53 class A motorhome.

All systems can be installed or shipped.

MasterCard VISA DISCOVER

Internet addresses:
HTTH:\\RVUSA.COM\RVPARTS\JARDINE\JARDINE\HTML
102200.1463@COMPUSEV.COM

WYOMING

12 TETON PASS elev. 8429'
(on Wyoming Highway 22 west of Jackson, WY)

A paved mountain pass with 10% grades is uncommon. Teton Pass has sustained 10% grades on both sides of the summit. Another unusual feature is that both *runaway truck ramps* on the east side of the pass can be used only if the runaway truck *crosses the oncoming lane of traffic.* There is a posted weight limit of 60,000 lbs. on this pass.

The westbound descent from the summit of Teton Pass begins with a 25 mph speed limit and a truck warning sign--**"Steep grade--10% next 3 miles--use lower gear."** This grade warning is repeated a mile later. About 2 1/2 miles down from the summit the grade eases to **6-7%** and the speed limit increases. This **grade continues for about 3-4 miles** and eases near the Idaho state line.

The eastbound descent from the summit of Teton Pass starts with a truck warning sign--**"Steep grade--10% next 5 1/2 miles--use lower gear."** There are 20 mph curves near the top. About 1/3 mile down from the summit is a sign--**"Runaway truck ramp--2 1/2 miles LEFT side."** This warning is repeated several times as you approach the ramp. To use the ramp you must cross the oncoming lane of traffic. The ramp slopes uphill.

The *second runaway truck ramp is about 1 mile after the first.* It, too, is on the **left side** and is an upsloping ramp. At this point the grade begins to ease to about 6-7% and the speed limit increases. The hill continues to the town of Wilson which is about 5 1/2 miles from the summit.

13 TOGOWOTEE PASS elev. 9658'
(on US 26/287 easts of Moran, WY)

The summit of Togwotee Pass is also the Continental Divide. The summit is about 22 miles east of the junction of US 89/191 and US 26/287. This junction is about 6800' in elevation or about 2850' lower than the summit. Most of this drop in elevation is in the first 17 miles west of the summit.

There is a truck warning sign at the summit for westbound traffic--**"6% grade next 17 miles."** It is a 6% descent but it is not steady. There are rolling hills most of the way down. About 8 miles down from the summit there is a truck warning sign--**"6% grade next 9 miles"** and a brake check turnout. These grade and length warnings are repeated every mile or two. It is a good 2 lane road with some 40 and 50 mph curves.

The eastbound descent begins with a truck warning sign--**"2-6% grade next 9 miles--use lower gear." The first 4 miles are fairly steady 5-6%** downhill with continuous 45 mph curves. The next 5 to 6 miles are stairstepping with the downhill sections still in the 5% range.

14 thru 17 see New Info on page 119

ADDITIONAL INFORMATION concerning grades.

Some readers have called to ask questions such as "What is a 6% grade? How do you define that?" We are not highway engineers but the answer is not difficult after you understand the concept. For every 100 feet of level roadway, a rise or fall of 6 feet would be a 6% grade. A rise or fall of 7 feet would be a 7% grade. A rise or fall of 10 feet would be a 10% grade, etc.

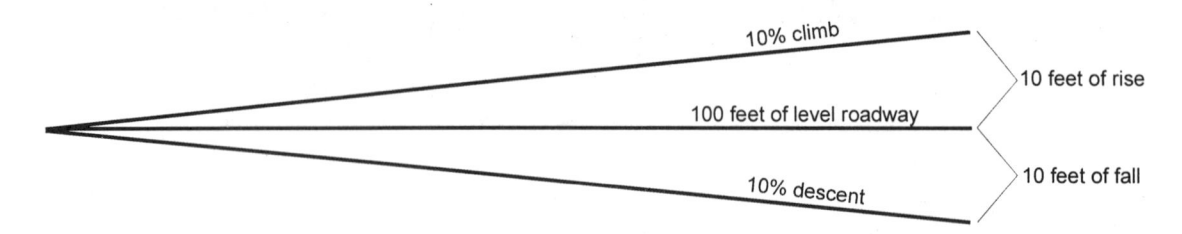

```
                              10% climb
                                              10 feet of rise
                         100 feet of level roadway
                              10% descent
                                              10 feet of fall
```

There are 5280 feet per mile so a 10% grade would be a rise or fall of 528 feet per mile. This would be 52.8 feet for each 1% of grade. The following table would result (with numbers rounded off).

528' of rise or fall in one mile is a	10% grade
476'	9%
422'	8%
370'	7%
317'	6%
264'	5%
211'	4%
158'	3%
105'	2%
53'	1%

For example, Cloudcroft Hill in New Mexico is a 4315' change in elevation spread over 16 miles. This works out to an average of just over 5% for the entire 16 miles. (4315' divided by 16 = 270' per mile or 5+%.) This is a very dangerous descent because of the combination of length and grade.

READER INPUT concerning grades not included in earlier editions of this book.

As stated in the introduction, the area covered by **Mountain Directory** is so large that we probably missed some grades that deserve to be included in the book. If you have knowledge of such grades, feel free to write or call and let us know the approximate length, percentage of grade, location, highway number, direction of travel, and landmarks (such as towns or rest areas, highway junctions, mile markers, etc.)

Hills that are only a mile or two long probably won't be included because there are simply too many of them and they usually don't present a problem during descent because they are too short to cause overheating of the brakes. In most cases, the mountain passes and steep grades that we included in the first editions were those that are long enough and steep enough to be of concern to drivers of heavy vehicles during the descent. Generally speaking, any grades over two or three miles long and 5% grade or more are worthy of consideration.

The purpose of this book is to try to eliminate surprises for the drivers of heavy vehicles. Any information that makes mountain driving safer is welcome. If you have such information please write or call: R & R Publishing Inc.
PO Box 941
Baldwin City, KS 66006-0941

1-800-594-5999

NEW PASS & GRADE INFORMATION contributed by readers.

The following information has been contributed by readers. We have not personally driven the hills in this list and don't know all of the details about them but we are told they are hills with significant grades. When possible we have obtained additional information from local highway departments. Some of these grades are minimal and some of them are quite serious. Local inquiry should be made. The number at the left of the page corresponds with the new numbers and symbols (▲) on the map and index pages in each state section.

ARIZONA

21 **Arizona: state highway 88** is a winding road with a 6 mile 7% northbound descent into Roosevelt. There are also two summits with 9% grades lasting about 2-3 miles on each side. These are between Globe and the last descent into Roosevelt. Two lane road with 20 & 25 mph curves.

22 **Arizona: US 89 Alt.** includes a summit at Jacob Lake which is north of the Grand Canyon. The grade is reported to be about 6% for about 7 miles on each side of the summit. No escape ramps.

NORTHERN CALIFORNIA

27 **California: state highway 1** between Leggett and Fort Bragg is reported to be narrow & winding with 10-15 mph curves & short 7% grades. Not suitable for large vehicles; logging trucks present.

28 **California: state highway 20** between Willits and Noyo. (north of Ukiah)

29 **California: state highway 49** between Auburn & Oakhurst. Narrow two lane; short steep grades.

30 **California: US highway 101.** The road from Redway to Shelter Cove is reported to include some long 7-8% grades. Most maps show it as a gravel road, but it is paved.

31 **California: US highway 101** south of Crescent City. Steady northbound descent, 3-4 miles long, approximately 6-7%. Also, **101** north of Orick has some 6-7% grades for several miles. Between Eureka and Ukiah **101** has many short 6% ups and downs and many curves but it is not as narrow.

32 **California: state highway 120** west of Yosemite National Park (near Chinese Camp).

33 **California: state highways 175 and 29** south of Clear Lake (north of Santa Rosa) may have grades as steep as 11%.

34 **California: US highway 199** between Crescent City and Grants Pass, OR. Some short 6-7% hills. Very narrow and winding in places.

SOUTHERN CALIFORNIA

20 **California: S3** between Borrego Springs and highway 78. Three miles of 5-6% on both sides of the hill. Called Yaqui Pass.

21 **California: I-10** between Indio and the rest area about 13 miles to the east. The grade is about 4-5%, and although it is not steady, hot weather makes this a difficult eastbound climb for many vehicles. Water is available at several places along the way. The grade is long enough to overheat brakes on the westbound descent from the rest area. The hill continues almost to Indio.

22 **California: highway S22** between Escondido and the Salton Sea. Two lane, 25 mph curves, 11 mile 5-10% eastbound descent between mileposts 17 and 6. The bottom of the hill is at Borrego Springs. Called Montezuma Grade. No escape ramps. Reported to be a 3550' drop in elevation in 11 miles for an average grade of just over 6%. **This is a serious hill, use caution.** (See California S3 above.)

23 **California: state highway 62** between Yucca Valley and Palm Springs. Reportedly fairly steep descent the first 4 miles south of Yucca Valley then gradual descent 4 miles to Morongo Valley. First 3 miles south of Morongo Valley steeper and then more gradual for 7 miles to Palm Springs. Mostly 4 lane.

24 **California: state highway 74** between Lake Elsinore and San Juan Capistrano. Moderate grades, many sharp turns and hairpins, some of which are being improved in 1996. Truck traffic.

25 **California: state highway 78** between Escondido and the Salton Sea. An eastbound descent just east of Julian with length restrictions due to sharp switchbacks. Grade is approximately 6 miles of

(NEW PASS & GRADE INFORMATION continued)

6%, narrow two lane, and no escape ramps. Called Banner Grade. Eastbound traffic can avoid this hill by going north on 79 highway at Santa Ysabel and then south on S2 to 78 highway.

26   **California: US highway 101** between Atascadero and San Luis Obispo. Cuesta Grade is a descent for southbound traffic at 6-7% for about 3 miles.

27   **California: state highway 152** from highway 101 in Gilroy to I-5 near Los Banos. Heavy commercial traffic. Long grades-approx. 5 miles west side and 8-10 miles east side. No escape ramps. Not too steep. Called Pacheco Pass.

28   **California: state highway 155** includes Greenhorn Summit between Woody and Lake Isabella. **Use extreme caution during the eastbound descent. Many vehicle fires and brake failures reported because grade is 4 miles of 11 % followed by 4 miles of 13% on curvy, two lane road. 3600' drop in elevation in 8 miles. No escape ramps.** Stop sign at the bottom of the grade. Severe winter conditions Nov. to Feb. Westbound descent includes short steep sections.

29   **California: state highway 178** between Bakersfield and US 395 includes Walker Pass (just west of state highway 14 junction.) The eastbound descent is about **8-10 miles of 5% grade with an escape ramp** on the right side near the bottom. Eastbound descent fairly straight while westbound descent is curvy with 15 mph switchback and shorter grade. Eastbound travelers between Bakersfield and Lake Isabella need to watch for overhanging rock. **Damage to trucks and motorhomes is common along this road.**

30   **California: state highway 198** between I-5 and US 101 (through Coalinga).

31   **California: state highway 198** in Sequoia National Park. **Very long and steep southbound descent from Giant Forest toward Three Rivers. Reported to be a drop of 5000' in 16 miles for an average of 6%. About 250 curves and hairpins in the 16 mile descent. Many brake failures reported on this road. No escape ramps.** Highway 180 northwest toward Fresno is not as bad.

32   **California: state highway 243** between Banning and Mountain Center.

COLORADO

45   **Colorado: US highway 24** between Minturn and Redcliff. (south of I-70 near Vail)

46   **Colorado: state highway 92** between Hotchkiss and Blue Mesa Reservoir is narrow in places with sharp drop-offs on the side and some steep grades.

47   **Colorado: state highway 96** between Silver Cliff and Greenwood. May have grades as steep as 8%. Called Hardscrabble Pass.

48   **Colorado: state highway 119** between Boulder and Nederland may have very steep grades.

49   **Colorado: US highway 160** descends at about 6% for about 4-5 miles as you enter Durango from the west. There are shorter 6% hills farther west that are eastbound climbs, westbound descents.

IDAHO

21   **Idaho: US 26** between Alpine Jct and Ririe may include several 6% grades but they are not long.

22   **Idaho: state highway 71** between Cambridge and Brownlee Dam the grades are said to be moderate but if you travel north of the dam, the last few miles into Cuprum are dirt road and very steep. The Idaho state map calls it Kleinschmidt Grade and says to inquire locally before attempting the grade.

23   **Idaho: US 89** between Geneva and Montpelier, ID. Geneva Pass, elev. 6982, is reported to be an eastbound descent of about 4 miles with 6 & 7% grade, switchbacks and no pullouts.

NEVADA

33   **Nevada: state highway 160** between Las Vegas and Pahrump includes Mountain Springs Summit which is 20 miles west of I-15. The eastbound descent toward Las Vegas is 7% for 5 miles. The westbound descent is 4% for 9 miles. No escape ramps; narrow two lane with climbing lane in the steep sections.

(**NEW PASS & GRADE INFORMATION** continued)

NEW MEXICO

13 This grade is actually in Texas but those traveling between El Paso and Carlsbad should know that **US highway 62/180** includes a very steep descent for westbound traffic. It is several miles long and it is between Nickel Creek and Pine Springs. This is a very steep climb for eastbound traffic, especially in the hot Texas summer.

OREGON

47 **Oregon: state highway 6** includes an eastbound descent between Lee's Camp and Glenwood. It is about 8-9% for a couple of miles.

48 **Oregon: US 101** between Lincoln City and Neskowin includes a summit near Cascade Head. The grade is 8-9% for 2-3 miles on each side of the hill. Also, the county road between Pacific City and Netarts, called the "Three Senics Route" includes a summit near Cape Lookout with grades from 6 to 12% for about 2 miles on both sides of the hill. The loop up to Cape Mears includes short grades in the 8-10% range. Whenever your map shows a "Cape" along the coast, there is a good chance of short, steep grades.

UTAH

14 **Utah: state highway 30** near Bear Lake in northern Utah. One mile south of Laketown a 4 mile 7% climb begins for those traveling south on this narrow, rough, winding road. Numerous 20 mph curves. There is a brake check area at the top of this hill and then a long gradual descent to Sage Jct.

15 **Utah: US highway 89** near Bear Lake in northern Utah. Southbound climb from Garden City to summit is about 3 miles of 6-8% grade with switchbacks. Southbound descent from summit includes many miles of 4-5% grade through Logan Canyon and into the town of Logan, UT.

WYOMING

14 **Wyoming: state highway 28**. South Pass is about midway between Lander and Farson. The grades on South Pass are not too bad but this pass has a reputation for wicked winter weather. Also there are two 4 mile eastbound descents between South Pass and the junction with US 287. One of these is 5-6% for 4 miles and the other is 7% for 4 miles. There are also several 5-6% hills about a mile long.

15 **Wyoming: US 191**. For southbounders there is a 4 mile 6% descent about halfway between I-80 and the Wyoming/Utah state line. There is a sharp curve to the right at the bottom of the grade.

16 **Wyoming: state highway 230** includes a 7 mile 7% eastbound descent into Woods Landing. There are at least two sharp turns and an escape ramp near the bottom of the hill. All two lane.

17 **Wyoming: state highway 530** south of Green River. There is a 5 mile 7% descent as you enter Green River from the south. It is a good two lane road with passing lanes. Going south from the top of this hill there are rolling hills for several miles and then a 3 mile 5% descent.

British Columbia and Texas do not have sections with maps in this book but the following information may be useful when traveling these areas.

BRITISH COLUMBIA

British Columbia: highway 3 westbound descent out of Osoyoos which is just north of Washington border on US 97.

British Columbia: highway 5 may have some very steep and long grades south of Kamloops.

TEXAS

Texas: US highway 62/180 south of Carlsbad, NM (between Nickel Creek and Pine Springs). This hill is a descent for westbound traffic. It is very steep and several miles long.

Texas: state highway 170 going into Big Bend National Park may have short grades as steep as 15%. Also, we understand there may be length restrictions on 170 between Lajitas and Presidio because of tight curves.